Common Formative Assessment

A TOOLKIT FOR PROFESSIONAL LEARNING COMMUNITIES AT WORK™

Kim Bailey & Chris Jakicic

Solution Tree | Press

a division of

Solution Tree

555 North Morton Street
Bloomington, IN 47404
800.733.6786 (toll free) / 812.336.7700

FAX: 812.336.7790
email: info@solution-tree.com
solution-tree.com

Visit **go.solution-tree.com/assessment** to download the reproducibles in this book.

Printed in the United States of America

15 14 13 12   3 4 5

FSC
www.fsc.org
MIX
Paper from
responsible sources
FSC® C011935

Library of Congress Cataloging-in-Publication Data

Bailey, Kim.
  Common formative assessment : a toolkit for professional learning communities at Work™ / Kim Bailey and Chris Jakicic.
       p. cm.
  Includes bibliographical references and index.
   ISBN 978-1-936765-14-0 (perfect bound) -- ISBN 978-1-936765-16-4 (library edition)
  1. Educational tests and measurements. 2. Professional learning communities. 3. Teaching teams. I. Jakicic, Chris. II. Title.
   LB3051.B32 2012
   371.26--dc23
                              2011032259

Solution Tree
Jeffrey C. Jones, CEO & President

Solution Tree Press
President: Douglas M. Rife
Publisher: Robert D. Clouse
Vice President of Production: Gretchen Knapp
Managing Production Editor: Caroline Wise
Senior Production Editor: Suzanne Kraszewski
Proofreader: Sarah Payne-Mills
Text Designer: Amy Shock
Cover Designer: Jenn Taylor

ACKNOWLEDGMENTS

Our journey to understanding how powerful common formative assessment practices are to improving student achievement has been significantly influenced by the opportunities we've had to learn from and work with Rick and Becky DuFour and Bob Eaker. We are most grateful to them for sharing not only their thinking and expertise, but also their commitment to quality education on behalf of children. We thank the people at Solution Tree for guiding us throughout the process of writing and revising this book. We especially want to thank our editor, Suzanne Kraszewski, for helping add all the important details that were needed to make this book more meaningful to teachers. Your work was most appreciated.

Throughout my years as an educator, I've been blessed to learn from many along the way who graciously shared their expertise and supported my personal and professional growth. From masterful teachers, to inspirational leaders, they shared "pearls of wisdom" that helped shape my passion for this work. My colleagues at Capistrano Unified School District, past and present, are at the top of this list, particularly my mentor, Austin Buffum. Thank you for believing in me, stretching my thinking, and for adding to those pearls of wisdom—they've now grown into a full strand that I can wear in all I do. Finally, I want to thank my entire family for their love, support, and patience throughout this project, especially my husband, Randy, who inspires me on a daily basis, and without whom, any accomplishment would be meaningless.

—Kim Bailey

Learning about common formative assessments and how to make them work for students as well as teachers has been a journey for me. I started learning from the terrific teachers at Woodlawn Middle School in Long Grove, Illinois. My journey continued as I worked with hundreds of teachers across the United States, designing and using assessments to make a difference for the students in their schools. While I can't possibly name all the teachers who have contributed to my learning, I do want to specifically mention Lisa May, third-grade teacher at Ivy Hall Elementary School in Buffalo Grove, Illinois; Gwen Flaskamp, English/language arts teacher at Twin Groves Middle School in Buffalo Grove, Illinois; and Vera Jones, former biology teacher and current administrator at Michigan City High School in Michigan City, Indiana. Each of these teachers has provided me with multiple examples of what works and what doesn't work in the real world of teaching and assessing. Your input has truly been enlightening. Jeanne Spiller, director of staff development in Kildeer School District 96, is my learning partner and the only other person I know who understands when I say, "I'm in love with the Common Core Standards." Finally, thanks to my husband, John, for listening to me talk endlessly about assessment. I really do love you more than the Common Core!

—Chris Jakicic

Solution Tree Press would like to thank the following reviewers:

Sean DeWeese
Science Teacher
Decatur High School
Decatur, Georgia

Mara Dumond
Educational Specialist
Institute of Teaching and Learning, CREC
Hartford, Connecticut

Donald Gross
School Board, Galloway Township Public Schools
Little Egg Harbor, New Jersey

Jana Loge
Southwest Missouri PLC Specialist
Southwest Missouri Professional Development Center
Springfield, Missouri

Jay Roth
Southwest Missouri PLC Specialist
Southwest Missouri Professional Development Center
Springfield, Missouri

Laurie Smith
Educational Data Consultant
Ottawa Area Intermediate School District
Holland, Michigan

Mark Tavernier
Director of Teaching and Learning
Clarke County School District
Athens, Georgia

TABLE OF CONTENTS

Reproducible pages are in italics.
Visit **go.solution-tree.com/assessment** to download the reproducibles in this book.

ABOUT THE AUTHORS ix

FOREWORD xi

INTRODUCTION 1

CHAPTER 1

Getting Started as a Collaborative Team 3

    The Big Ideas of a Professional Learning Community 3

    The Role of Teams in a PLC 5

    The Nuts and Bolts of Working as a Team 5

    Where Do We Start? 10

    Full Speed Ahead 12

CHAPTER 2

Setting the Stage for Common Formative Assessments 13

    Formative Versus Summative Assessment 14

    What Does *Common* Mean? 16

    Benefits of Common Assessments 16

    Putting It Together 18

    A Balanced Assessment System 19

    Do We Have Time to Do It All? 23

    Grading Practices 23

    Gathering and Collecting Data 24

CHAPTER 3

Power Standards—The Essential Outcomes 27

Moving From Individual to Team Decisions 28
Defining *Most Important* 29
Achieving Clarity About Standards Vocabulary 30
What Makes Learning *Essential*? 30
Aligning the Power Standards 33
Where Do the Common Core State Standards Fit In? 34
Time Is an Important Factor 35
Schoolwide or Districtwide Power Standards? 35
Use, Review, and Rewrite 36

CHAPTER 4

The Unwrapping Process—Achieving Collective Clarity on Learning Targets 37

Looking at the Structure of Your Standards 38
Unwrapping the Standards 40
Getting Started as a Team 46
We've Unwrapped Our Standards—Now What? 47

CHAPTER 5

Designing Quality Common Formative Assessments 49

Step One: Decide What to Assess 50
Step Two: Decide How to Assess 51
Step Three: Develop the Assessment Plan 53
Step Four: Determine the Timeline 56
Step Five: Write the Assessment 56
Step Six: Review the Assessment Before Administration 60
Step Seven: Set Proficiency Criteria and Decide How to Gather the Data 60
Final Thoughts 61

CHAPTER 6

The Big Picture—Pacing Guides and Unit Design 63

From Isolated Standards to an Instructional Roadmap 64
Developing a Pacing Guide 64
Backward Planning of Specific Units 68
Designing Instruction for 21st Century Skills 71
Final Thoughts 72

CHAPTER 7

Now What? Using Data to Make a Difference 73

Step One: Gathering the Data 74
Step Two: Analyzing the Data 75
Step Three: Planning the Response 76
Step Four: Reviewing the Assessment 79
Step Five: Next Steps 80
Final Thoughts 82

CHAPTER 8

Getting the Most Bang for Your Assessment Buck—Involving Students 83

Help Students Know What They Will Learn and Why 85
Engage Students in Defining Quality Work 86
Focus on Timely, Effective Feedback and Self-Reporting—Not Grades 87
Partner With Students to Monitor Their Progress and Communicate Their Strengths and Weaknesses 88
Final Thoughts 89

CHAPTER 9

Sustaining the Work 91

Remain Focused on the Why 92
Reflect on All the Benefits of Using Common Formative Assessments 92
Provide or Seek Support for Teams 92
Build Capacity to Lead the Work 93
Remember That Experience Yields Efficiency 94
Be Attentive to Both Immediate and Systemic Learning 94
Celebrate Successes 95
A Call to Action 96

APPENDIX

Tools for Teams 97

Work Cycle for Teams. *98*
SMART Goals and Action Planning Worksheet *100*
Balanced Assessment System Framework *101*
Sample Agenda for Determining Power Standards *102*
Sample Agenda for Unwrapping Standards *103*
Unwrapping Template *104*

Unwrapping Template for Backward Planning *105*

Evaluating the Quality of an Assessment *106*

Sample Protocol for Developing an Assessment *107*

Assessment Plan *108*

Pacing Guide Template *109*

Backward Planning Unit Design Template *110*

Data Team Meeting Template *112*

Protocol for Data Team Meeting *115*

Student-Involved Assessment Worksheet *116*

Short-Term Cycle *117*

Long-Term Cycle *118*

Considerations for the Future *119*

REFERENCES AND RESOURCES 121

INDEX 127

ABOUT THE AUTHORS

Kim Bailey is director of staff development and instructional support for the Capistrano Unified School District in southern California. Her leadership has been instrumental in uniting and guiding educators throughout the district's fifty-six schools in their journey to becoming professional learning communities (PLCs). In addition to her role at Capistrano, Kim works with schools and districts across the nation, providing guidance and support to move forward with their own development as PLCs. Kim is passionate about empowering teams to do the important work inherent in effective learning communities, including the development of common formative assessments and the alignment of standards, assessment, interventions, and instruction.

Kim's education background spans over thirty years, and her work at Capistrano has won national praise. The National School Boards Association (NSBA) recognized Kim's leadership in coordinating and implementing the district's Professional Development Academies. The academies received the distinguished *American School Board Journal* Magna Award and the California School Boards Association Golden Bell Award. She has also taught courses in educational leadership as an adjunct faculty member at Chapman University in Orange, California, and she is coauthor of *Starting Strong: Surviving and Thriving as a New Teacher.*

To learn more about Kim's work, visit http://kbailey4learning.wordpress.com. Follow her on Twitter @bailey4learning.

Chris Jakicic, EdD, served as principal of Woodlawn Middle School in Long Grove, Illinois, from its opening day in 1999 through the spring of 2007. Under her leadership, the staff shifted toward a collaborative culture focused on learning and implemented assessment *for* learning practices to shape their instructional strategies. Student motivation and performance also increased. Chris began her career teaching middle school science before serving as principal of Willow Grove Elementary in Buffalo Grove, Illinois, for nine years. Her experience as a practitioner guides her work with schools; she wants teachers to feel confident that they have the skills and the ability to make a difference for their students.

Through her work with teachers and administrators across the country, Chris emphasizes that effective teaming is the heart of PLCs. She also shares practical knowledge about how to use data conversations to interpret classroom information for effective instruction.

Chris has written articles for the *Journal of Staff Development* and *Illinois School Research and Development Journal* detailing her experiences with common assessments and PLCs. She has worked as an adjunct instructor at National-Louis University as well as Loyola University Chicago, where she earned a doctor of education.

To learn more about Chris, visit her on the web at www.chrisjakicic.com, or follow her on Twitter @cjakicic.

To book Kim or Chris for professional development, contact pd@solution-tree.com.

FOREWORD

By Richard DuFour and Rebecca DuFour

When *Professional Learning Communities at Work*™ was published in 1998, we made the following fundamental assertion in its opening sentence: "the most promising strategy for sustained and substantive school improvement is developing the capacity of school personnel to function as a professional learning community" (DuFour & Eaker, 1998, p. xi). In the years since that publication, researchers from around the world have supported our conclusion, the professional organizations of teachers and administrators have endorsed the PLC at Work™ process, and a steadily increasing number of schools and entire districts have demonstrated the power of the PLC at Work process to promote higher levels of learning both for students and the adults who serve them.

Unfortunately, despite the growing evidence of the power of PLCs, many educators continue to engage in a superficial application of the process. Some educators have merely changed the letterhead on their school stationery or hung banners declaring their school to be a PLC, even though they do none of the things that members of a true PLC actually do. Others are content to read and discuss the same book and pretend that participating in a book club means they are operating as a PLC. In some schools, educators meet on a weekly basis to discuss issues that have little impact on student achievement, and then they return to business as usual in their isolated classrooms.

But those faculties that commit to implementing the PLC process at a deep rather than superficial level—a commitment that requires significant changes in traditional practices—inevitably find the need for greater and greater specificity as they move further into the process. They go beyond declaring themselves to be PLCs and instead embrace the three big ideas of the process: (1) the mission of our school must shift from ensuring that students are taught to ensuring that all students learn at high levels, (2) we must break down the traditional walls of isolation and work collaboratively and collectively if we are to fulfill that purpose, and (3) we must shift our focus from activities and use actual evidence of student learning to improve our individual and collective practice and better meet the needs of our individual students.

These faculties challenge themselves to implement actionable steps to bring the three big ideas to life. They recognize that asserting that they are committed to high levels of learning for all students is a hollow statement unless they work together to clarify exactly what students will be expected to learn. They understand that to enhance their effectiveness in the classroom they must gather evidence of each student's learning on a timely basis and use the results to inform and improve their individual and collective practice. They acknowledge that in virtually every instructional unit some students will experience initial difficulty in learning and therefore their schools must develop a systematic process to provide those students with extra time and support for learning. They understand that assessment can help them to identify students who are highly proficient and thus need opportunities for enrichment and extension of their learning.

While each of these actionable steps is supported by research and just makes sense, educators who reach this stage of implementation inevitably find the need for increasing specificity as they move forward. Questions they confront are likely to include the following:

- How should we organize teachers into teams?

- How can we help teams establish effective collaborative processes?

- How can we build trust among members of a team?

- How can we effectively address conflict among members of a team?

- What is the best process for helping a team establish a guaranteed curriculum with clear learning targets that ensure all students have access to the same essential knowledge and skills regardless of the teacher to whom they are assigned?

- What are the elements of an effective assessment process in a PLC, and how can members of collaborative teams develop their assessment literacy?

- What are the different kinds of assessments, and what purpose does each serve?

- What are the elements of effective common formative assessments, and why do these assessments play such an important role in the PLC process?

- How can we use the results of the assessment process to expand our individual and collective instructional expertise?

- How can we use the results of the assessment process to respond to the individual needs of students?

- How can we involve students in monitoring their own learning and using assessments to build on their learning?

- How can we sustain continuous improvement?

These are the nuts-and-bolts issues that every faculty will encounter on its road to becoming a PLC. Fortunately for those schools, Kim Bailey and Chris Jakicic have developed a powerful toolkit for addressing those very predictable issues in ways that will drive the PLC at Work process deeper into the school culture. *Common Formative Assessment: A Toolkit for Professional Learning Communities at Work*™ is aptly named. It truly is a toolkit for PLCs. In fact, it is one of the best toolkits for collaborative teams of educators committed to the PLC process that we have encountered. It provides the specificity and insights that can only come from authors who have not only led the PLC at Work process in their own school districts but have also helped schools at all levels, in a variety of different settings, overcome the challenges inherent in deep implementation.

Kim and Chris demonstrate that their recommendations are based on solid educational research, but this book is clearly written by practitioners for practitioners. The authors do not ask educators to become psychometricians or statisticians, but they do ask them to work with their colleagues and collectively reflect about their professional practice. They challenge educators to use assessment not merely to give students the chance to prove what they have *learned* but to *improve* on their *learning*. And most importantly, they provide the tools and techniques to help educators meet that challenge.

Common Formative Assessment presents a compelling case for engaging educators in the kind of work that actually leads to improved student achievement. It is filled with wisdom that we urge you to take to heart. Follow Kim and Chris's advice and you, too, can help the educators or collaborative teams of educators in your PLC school and district shift their focus from lesson planning to learning planning.

INTRODUCTION

Teachers around the world are organizing into collaborative teams and getting excited about their school or district becoming a professional learning community. During our work with these teams, we are often asked for assurance that they are doing things the right way. Team members want to know what steps to take, what to talk about, and what materials they should use. Our answer is always the same: there is no one right way to do the work that high-performing teams do. The process of becoming a PLC is a journey that takes time, and each team's journey is different from that of other teams. We do, however, remind teams that their work should be about student learning. We also remind them that in order to increase student achievement, they will need to learn together about new strategies and processes as teachers, assessment authors, and team members.

We emphasize that the catalyst for real change—real improvement in student achievement—is writing and implementing common formative assessments. During this process, team members have collaborative conversations about what their standards mean, what proficiency looks like, and how best to assure all students learn. Teams engaged in designing, using, and responding to common formative assessments become more knowledgeable about their standards, more assessment literate, and better able to develop more strategies for helping all students learn.

Although we respond that there is no one right way to write and use common formative assessments, most teams still seek a practical resource to guide them in their journey. They want to review templates and protocols while they build proficiency and become more confident in this work. So we decided to create a toolkit of ideas, templates, and protocols that teams can use as a launching pad into this work. We believe that it is important for teams to understand that these are only jump-start resources—in the end, teams will likely create better products for their own work than the products we've included here. Your team should modify and improve the templates we provide and make them its own.

This resource can be used by teams at varying levels of implementation in the assessment process. Teams that are just beginning the process of building common formative assessments can move through each chapter in order to become proficient in the entire process. Teams that are further along on their journey can reference and use each chapter independently.

When writing this book, we focused on making it practitioner friendly, but we also made sure the strategies and recommendations we provide are grounded in research and best practices. To that end, we cite both formal research and information from individuals viewed as experts in the field.

This book's nine chapters each focus on one part of the assessment process. Chapter 1 is a primer on the PLC journey. It provides an overview and explanation about how common formative assessments fit into the work of teams and the framework that teams might follow to become truly collaborative. Chapter 2 explains the nature of a balanced assessment system within schools or districts, the roles that each type of assessment serves in support of student learning and continuous improvement, and how to design an assessment system to ensure that teachers use both formative and summative assessment data in the best ways possible. In chapter 3, we explain the foundational work of identifying and using power standards as the beginning point for common formative assessments.

Chapter 4 explains the important first step in assessment design. It guides teams through the process of unwrapping their power standards to reveal clear learning targets of instruction—the targets that will not only be taught but also assessed formatively. These targeted and monitored skills, strategies, and concepts will guide teams to know what to do next with students who need more help. Chapter 5 further explores the strategies of assessment design. What kinds of assessments make good formative assessments, and how do we write those assessments so that the data are the right information to help teams know what to do next for their students? Chapter 6 discusses how teams plan their instruction with common formative assessments in mind. It provides examples of how teams might plan a unit to create planned time for both meaningful assessment as well as embedded response time based on the information these assessments provide.

Chapter 7 looks at how teams use the data they gather to know specifically how to help students experiencing difficulty and how to help identify students who have already learned the material and can benefit from enrichment instruction. Because we know that students benefit when included in the assessment process, chapter 8 explores ways that teachers can assure student involvement. Finally, chapter 9 puts all of the pieces together to lay out an adult-learning cycle teams can use to connect the dots of their work as they implement this process.

As you begin this important work, we hope that you will feel confident that common formative assessment will make a difference for your students. By focusing on student learning, and by using this process, your own learning will increase. We *know* that this is the right work. The research is compelling, and the results are impressive! Be willing to try the process knowing that everything won't be perfect the first time. *Doing* will lead to *learning*.

CHAPTER 1

Getting Started as a Collaborative Team

If you're reading this book, there's a good chance you and your team are familiar with the Professional Learning Communities at Work concept put forth by Richard DuFour, Robert Eaker, and Rebecca DuFour. However, in case you are not, we will begin by reviewing the big ideas related to PLCs and what it takes to function in effective collaborative teams. We'll discuss the elements of PLCs, as well as some critical strategies and processes that your collaborative team will rely on while building its effectiveness. This review will help clarify the big picture of PLCs, build new knowledge, explore the types of strategies that will help prepare teams for the work of designing and using of common formative assessments, and simply provide some good reminders of what effective teams do. You can explore much of the information within this chapter in greater detail in publications such as *Revisiting Professional Learning Communities at Work: New Insights for Improving Schools* (DuFour, DuFour, & Eaker, 2008), *Learning by Doing: A Handbook for Professional Learning Communities at Work*, second edition (DuFour, DuFour, Eaker, & Many, 2010a), *Raising the Bar and Closing the Gap: Whatever It Takes* (DuFour, DuFour, Eaker, & Karhanek, 2010), and *The Collaborative Teacher: Working Together as a Professional Learning Community* (Erkens et al., 2008). These resources have captured the essence of what it means to work as a PLC and can assist schools and districts as they dig into this important work.

The Big Ideas of a Professional Learning Community

PLCs are not a program, a fad, or a meeting. A PLC is a way of doing business in schools—and that business is learning. PLCs work with that end in mind. As defined by DuFour et al. (2010b, p. 4), a PLC is "an ongoing process in which educators work collaboratively in recurring cycles of collective inquiry and action research to achieve better results for the students they serve." PLCs, they continue, "operate under the assumption that the key to improved learning for students is continuous job-embedded learning for educators" (p. 4).

The term *professional learning community* describes a culture and structure now being employed by tens of thousands of schools and districts—not just across North America, but around the world. PLCs are based on the beliefs and practices of highly effective organizations and schools (Newmann & Wehlage, 1995; Senge, 1990) and characterized by three big ideas that guide their work (DuFour & Eaker, 2008):

1. **A focus on learning**—Schools that operate as PLCs have a constant eye on learning and will stop at nothing to ensure high levels of learning for all students. This commitment is shared across all members of the learning community and assumes that everyone will work together to examine and change instructional practices to make sure all students learn at high levels. Rather than view their role as serving only those students who are in their classroom, teachers assume collective responsibility for the learning of all students. As a result of this collective responsibility, the pathway for attaining high levels of learning isn't achieved through random acts of improvement implemented in isolation by individual teachers, but rather through systematic improvements that enhance the learning of all students.

2. **A culture of collaboration**—In a PLC, there is a collective commitment to *all* students in the school. The traditional line that divides "your" students versus "mine" evaporates into a culture of "our" students. Teams are responsible for the learning of all students, and in order to get there, everyone's efforts are pointed in the same direction. To that end, it's impossible for teachers working in isolation to ensure high levels of learning for all students. It's clear that the task is too great, and few, if any, teachers are equipped with all the knowledge or the energy to make it happen on their own. In a PLC, teacher teams collaborate to define what students need to know and do, monitor their learning, and respond systematically when students aren't learning essential concepts and skills. Teachers share their best instructional practices so that all students can benefit. Consequently, students receive a guaranteed and viable curriculum, one that's clearly defined and consistently delivered regardless of what teacher they have (Marzano, 2003). Their learning is the focus of an entire team, and they reap the expertise of all of its members in a systematic fashion.

3. **A focus on results**—In a PLC, there is a significant shift from a focus on *teaching* to a focus on *learning*. Merely discussing strategies or sharing best practices isn't enough. PLCs focus on the collective impact their professional practice has on student learning, and that impact is measured along the way by collecting and responding to meaningful data. DuFour (2004) says it best when he states that the mission "is not simply to ensure that students are taught but to ensure that they learn" (p. 1). The all-too familiar phrase "I taught it, they just didn't learn it" is the antithesis of PLCs. In PLCs, it's all about what students have learned—not what teachers have taught. This constant focus on results in student learning is the impetus for developing and using common formative assessments, as well as any subsequent interventions that provide students with additional time and support.

The Role of Teams in a PLC

According to DuFour, DuFour, and Eaker (2008), the engine behind school improvement in a professional learning community is the team—grade-level teams, departmental teams, or cross-departmental teams. The actions of these teams are guided by the following questions:

- What do we want students to know and do?

- How do we know they are learning?

- What do we do when they're not learning?

- How do we respond when they've already learned the information?

Simply put, the power of improvement lies within the team—"a group of people working *interdependently* to achieve a *common goal* for which members are held *mutually accountable*" (DuFour et al., 2010b, p. 6). The goal is to improve student learning, and teams are committed to examining and adjusting their practices so that all students walk away knowing and being able to do the things that are considered essential. The focus on a common goal is what differentiates a truly collaborative team within a PLC from a more traditional grade-level or course team. The ultimate focus of a collaborative team working within a PLC is placed squarely and consistently on student learning, not merely on the adult behaviors or the products they create. Effective teams have established a culture and a structure that enables them to do the work of clarifying their curriculum, identifying measures that monitor the learning of their students, intervening to ensure that students get needed additional time and support, and differentiating their instruction so that all students, no matter where they are, learn at high levels.

John Hattie (2009), in his book *Visible Learning: A Synthesis of Over 800 Meta-Analyses Relating to Achievement*, examines numerous instructional practices and concludes that teachers working together in collaborative teams to clarify what students must learn, gather evidence of learning, and analyze that evidence so that they can identify the most powerful teaching strategy is indeed the practice that yields the most results in improving student learning. Getting this powerful continuous improvement model in place requires both structural adjustments and cultural shifts.

The Nuts and Bolts of Working as a Team

Before you and your team can move forward with the work of creating and implementing common formative assessments, there are some foundational structures and processes to establish. Let's examine these key factors.

Time to Collaborate

The first, and perhaps most obvious, factor is that your team must have time to collaborate on a frequent basis. The work of developing common assessments is not something that can be accomplished simply by meeting as a team once each quarter or even once monthly. To build clarity and consistency across our classrooms so that all students learn at high levels, team members need to meet with a high level of regularity. Rather than collaborating periodically during isolated events, teams need to establish a work flow that connects their actions from meeting to meeting, with little time between.

Schools of all sizes and grade levels have identified a number of ways to find time during the instructional day so that teachers are empowered to collaborate. These include the restructuring of their instructional day, identifying common prep periods, conducting late-start or early-out schedules, and establishing periods of the week or day during which teacher teams can capture collaborative time. A number of additional ideas for finding time appear on the AllThingsPLC website (www.allthingsplc.info), a tremendous online resource that contains articles, blogs, and recommendations from people in the field who are successfully implementing PLCs. There are suggestions that apply to a number of types of teams, including grade-alike and course-alike teams, departmental teams (teaching similar content, but not necessarily the same course), and e-teams (electronic).

Clarity of Purpose and Commitment

Once your team has been defined and has established a structure for meeting on a frequent basis, it's critical to affirm your mission—your fundamental purpose. In a PLC, that mission is to improve student learning, and all members have a clear and collective understanding of the work to be done. There is not merely an individual commitment from each member of the team, but a team commitment for members to hold themselves accountable to that purpose. While your school may have worked through the process of clarifying its mission, vision, values, and goals, you need to purposefully transfer the conversation to the team level. We highly recommend taking the time to collectively answer these questions: Why do we exist as a collaborative team? What commitments do we make to accomplish this work? The answers will help define and focus your team's mission and unite members by establishing a formal commitment to place student learning at the core of all the team does. If your team hasn't extended that same clarity to its work, it risks the danger of getting off track, or veering off on a nonproductive tangent that's not focused on student learning.

A clear mission or purpose helps to guide team actions and the focus of every member. As a lighthouse guides ships through the fog, the clear purpose of working to improve student learning illuminates the intended course of teamwork. From time to time, teams may experience conversations that are challenging or processes that are unclear. Having that lighthouse that every member of the team can point to during those foggy times can keep teams on a path that is meaningful. In practice, some mature teams have set the expectation that their time will be focused on student learning. They hold themselves to this expectation by bringing evidence of student learning (such as assessment results or student work) to every meeting. They have clear agreement about what they must accomplish and hold each other accountable to stay the course toward that mission.

A Clear Picture of the Process

Effective teams in PLCs understand that there is a work flow inherent within the collaborative process. We recommend following a cycle of collective inquiry, sometimes referred to as the Plan, Do, Study, Act cycle (Deming, 1968), which embeds the use of data and reflective practices throughout. The model provides a structure for action research, provides a process to target an area for improvement, and identifies specific strategies for that improvement. During the implementation of those strategies, teams collect evidence along the way, and then collectively examine the results to determine their effectiveness as well as implications for further practice. Here's how it might play out for a team across a period of time:

1. **Plan**—Create an instruction and assessment plan. The team identifies the next instructional segment and the most essential learning or outcomes (power standards) to be addressed. They reflect on the data from prior assessments, or even the previous year, to determine if there

are any learning targets that were particularly challenging for students. After establishing a SMART goal (one that is strategic and specific, measurable, attainable, results oriented, and time bound; O'Neill & Conzemius, 2006), they discuss potential common formative assessment items and establish a timeline for their implementation.

2. **Do**—Execute the plan. The team implements the instructional plan and gathers data along the way through common formative assessments—assessments created collaboratively by a team of teachers from the same grade level or course.

3. **Study**—Study the results. Collectively, the team examines the results of its common formative assessments and identifies patterns that emerge, including common student errors and differences in results between classrooms.

4. **Act**—Take action. Armed with this new information, the team moves forward in providing brief, but powerful interventions that provide additional time and support for those students who did not attain the targeted skills and concepts. Additionally, team members might include in their teaching repertoire any successful strategies that they discovered when analyzing data with their colleagues.

The Work Cycle for Teams tool (page 98 in the Tools for Teams appendix) further describes the Plan, Do, Study, Act cycle and will help guide your team through this process. (Note: This cycle also includes a Prepare phase that relates to the development of team norms in preparation for collaborative work.)

Norms for Working Together

Team *norms* are agreed-on day-to-day behaviors—collective commitments—that the team will follow in order to work purposefully and productively. Norms define *how* each member of the team will function or act within the context of collaboration (DuFour, DuFour, Eaker, & Karhanek, 2010). Why is this important? Let's first think about what effective teams look like. Members of effective teams are able to navigate through a number of issues and remain professional and open to the input of their colleagues. They are respectful of differing opinions, and they work to build consensus, rather than overpowering opposing views. This does not happen without specifically defining *norms*—the way that every team member commits to doing business with other members of their team. Here are some examples of norms for collaborative teams:

- We will arrive prepared and on time.
- We will be participant members.
- We will stick to our focus on student learning during our meetings.
- We will listen to others' opinions respectfully and will use a consensus process.
- We will base our decisions on data.
- We will not blame the students.

Norms serve as an important vehicle to support the cultural shifts within your team or school from one in which teachers work in isolation, making all instructional decisions independently, to one in which teams work not just collaboratively but interdependently. In this collaborative culture, teachers must put aside their personal preferences and assumptions for the good of the whole team. Once these decisions cross the classroom door, their impact becomes much more imperative, and the reliance on the team's collective commitments will make or break how the decisions play out. Consider, for example, a teacher who is now required to change a favorite unit or shorten the time spent teaching a particular concept because the team has agreed to have students ready for a common formative assessment by a certain date. The norm for that team is that it will use consensus as a process for identifying actions within the team. If the teacher does not adhere to the agreement, she is breaking the norm, and the within-group accountability and trust is at risk.

If your team has not yet established its norms for working together, we encourage you to use the process outlined in *Learning by Doing* (DuFour et al., 2010a, pp. 137–138). If your team has already established its norms, we recommend that you review and refine them on a regular basis.

Consensus-Building Strategies

When teachers work together with their colleagues, there can be both positive energy and challenging moments. Teams are often faced with difficult conversations and differences of opinion. For example, in the midst of determining the best way to assess essential learnings, members of the team may express very clear preferences that disagree with those expressed by others. To harness that energy and direct it in a positive fashion, teams must employ a respectful decision-making process that keeps the basic tenets of effective collaboration in effect. DuFour et al.'s (2010b) definition of consensus captures the essence of this powerful process: "Consensus is achieved when (1) all points of view have not only been heard but also solicited, and (2) the will of the group is evident even to those who most oppose it" (p. 2). The consensus process is designed to identify solutions, but in a way that brings out critical information about each potential option being explored and weighs that option in an objective fashion. The process yields the best solution that's available to the team at that moment in time and is not based on meeting halfway or voting. The steps to building consensus include:

- **Step one**—Build shared knowledge (of the issue).
- **Step two**—Define the problem and determine any criteria that would need to be met in order for the solution to be considered acceptable. (For example, the solution can't increase costs, or it must be accomplishable during the instructional day.)
- **Step three**—Participate in guided brainstorming or input on solutions.
- **Step four**—Prune the solutions.
- **Step five**—Identify a solution that meets acceptability criteria.
- **Step six**—Establish final consensus.

When teams are working to reach consensus, it's important to assign various roles in support of the process. One of the most crucial roles is that of the facilitator. Facilitators are the emcees of the process and help the team move through the steps and adhere to the agreed-on course of action. They will also make adjustments as needed, such as taking a pause to restate what has already been agreed on, or restating the focus question. It's also helpful to have a recorder, a timekeeper, and someone to help monitor the norms.

Consider this scenario: A grade-level team is trying to decide how best to move forward with the results of its common formative assessments. The members each have different opinions about how best to provide corrective instruction based on the results. For example, one teacher thinks that each member should serve his or her own students, while another thinks students might be clustered and divided across the four classrooms at that grade level, with each teacher serving a group of students based on need. Rather than spinning off in various directions or raising angst about whose idea is better, the team members followed the steps to building consensus.

First, they affirmed their purpose for providing additional time and support to students who were struggling (step one). After examining the potential numbers of students who would need this support, they generated criteria for acceptability of their potential solutions (step two). One of their criteria supported the concept that the solution would enable team members to work efficiently without duplicating efforts. They then generated potential solutions for providing corrective instruction to their students (step three). During this time, the individuals proposing the solutions had the opportunity to clarify and answer questions from members of the group. During this time, however, members of the team were not allowed to *evaluate* solutions. After all ideas were exhausted, the team weighed each solution against its criteria for acceptability (steps four and five). The solution that was determined to meet the criteria most effectively was a hybrid solution: teachers would swap students twice weekly to receive differentiated instruction, including interventions, based on their common assessment results. To determine final consensus (step six), they used a Fist to Five strategy (see the following feature box for more details) to determine the level of comfort and commitment to implement the solution. In the end, the group felt that its ideas were heard and that the best decision was made that would support student needs.

Fist to Five is a quick strategy used in a variety of organizations to check a group's agreement with a proposed solution or concept (DuFour et al., 2010a). No materials or equipment are needed. Here's how it works. After stating the proposal, the facilitator asks individuals to react to a proposal by raising the number of fingers that correspond to their position:

- **5 fingers**—I'm all for the idea. I can be a leader.
- **4 fingers**—I'm for the idea. I can provide support.
- **3 fingers**—I'm not sure, but I am willing to trust the group's opinion.
- **2 fingers**—I'm not sure. I need more discussion.
- **1 finger**—I can't support it at this time. I need more information.
- **0 fingers (fist)**—No. I need an alternative that I can support.

When viewing a room of raised hands, it's important to read the room and get a sense of where the group lies in terms of its acceptance of a proposal. You may see a large amount of agreement, or you may see large variation in the number of fingers raised. Whoever is facilitating the conversation should acknowledge the level of agreement and make general statements such as, "It appears that most of the people here are willing to support this idea," if most hands are showing 4s and 5s. If a significant number of individuals are showing two or fewer fingers, there may need to be more discussion to understand the concerns.

Remember, however, the definition of consensus is *not* that everybody agrees. Rather, you have reached consensus when the *will of the group* is clearly evident, even to those who individually oppose it (DuFour et al., 2010a), and regardless of their opinion, they agree to move forward with the decision and not sabotage the implementation.

A Commitment and Process for Examining Results

It should be evident that a major premise in PLCs is that collaborative conversations take place around results and that those results are made transparent to all members of the team. Given this continuous focus on the examination of results in a PLC, teams must be comfortable working with data in a collective fashion. To that end, it's essential that teams examine their norms to ensure that they support collaboration around data. Having such norms provides parameters for discussing and examining data in a way that will lessen any potential for individuals to feel threatened or challenged. For example, a team norm might include the following: "We will examine our results without judgment, but with the interest of learning from each other," or "We will use evidence of our effectiveness to make continuous improvements in learning."

Additionally, teams will benefit greatly from using protocols to guide conversations around data. A *protocol* is simply an outline of steps and guidelines that helps teams structure productive conversations around such things as looking at student work, analyzing assessment results, or conducting lesson studies. There are a number of protocols available for use by teams, and many teams create their own. We highly recommend that teams take advantage of these to facilitate conversations throughout the process of not only looking at data but also for discussing instructional practices and calibrating the scoring of student work. A number of protocols are referenced and included in this book to assist teams.

Development of Purposeful Products

Effective teams have something to show for their collaborative time, and those products are purposeful. The products they create vary based on the current goals of the team, but may include items such as a listing of identified power standards, pacing guides, standards-aligned units, and products in support of common formative assessments, such as scoring rubrics. Not only do these products provide evidence of the team's collaboration, but they build momentum within the team in that they are meaningful and focused on student learning. A great reference for guiding teams through the process of creating critical and purposeful products is Critical Issues for Team Consideration in *Learning by Doing: A Handbook for Professional Learning Communities at Work* (DuFour et al., 2010a, pp. 130–131). Visit **go.solution-tree .com/assessment** to download this tool, which lists eighteen critical issues and a rating scale to evaluate where your team stands on the issues.

Where Do We Start?

Your team's goal is to hit the ground running and develop meaningful products that empower you toward continuous improvement in student learning. Following are strategies that help your team do just that. The overarching goal of each of these strategies is to focus and maximize the amount of time the team has to develop meaningful products, not to detract from that time. If your processes and systems are efficient and concise, they will help your team stay on track.

Prepare for Efficient and Focused Meetings

Chances are you've been at a meeting that was not well organized or efficient. What were your thoughts about attending another one? You were probably less than enthusiastic. Let's think about our team meetings. Don't we want those to be highly organized and efficient so that our time is well spent?

Of course! Here are some strategies that teams have found helpful for running organized and efficient team meetings:

- **Define roles**—It's important to establish roles for team meetings. These roles may include a meeting facilitator, the timekeeper, and a recorder. While roles may not be held by the same individual each meeting, it's a good idea to begin with the same person facilitating until the team matures and has built capacity for that role.

- **Have clear agendas and keep notes**—Meeting agendas should inform and guide whatever discussions will be taking place about student learning. In general, they will follow one or more steps of the Plan, Do, Study, Act cycle. Consider the sample in figure 1.1.

Meeting focus: Identify greatest area of need (GAN) in seventh-grade English language arts (writing), and develop quarterly SMART goal.

Agenda:

- Examine data from previous writing assessments to identify common areas of need based on grade-level writing rubric.

- Identify goal for improvement in specific learning target writing based on the findings.

- Write SMART goal and an action plan for accomplishment of the goal.

Next time: Create common formative assessment focused on identified learning targets.

Figure 1.1: Seventh-grade English language arts team meeting agenda.

As you can see, while not complicated, this agenda is clear about what the team will accomplish during members' time together. Additionally, the agenda includes a conversation about the team's next steps. Agendas and notes are helpful not only to ensure that there's productive work from meeting to meeting but to inform members of the team who were unable to attend. Recording notes throughout the meeting creates a group memory of conversations, decisions, and next steps that will carry forward the team's momentum through the next meeting. These notes should be shared with everyone on the team, and they will serve as a basis for creating the next agenda. They have an added benefit in that they help team members hold one another accountable for decisions made at each meeting.

- **Stay organized**—The work you will be doing as a collaborative team isn't necessarily linear, and at times, the paperwork may pile up. Meeting notes, assessment data, drafts of common formative assessments, and standards documents can end up in a mess, or worse yet, unavailable when they're needed in the midst of a team meeting. We highly recommend using data notebooks organized into critical sections. Ideally, each member of the team will have a copy of this notebook so that everyone can be on the same page (literally and figuratively!).

Focus Your Team's Efforts With Clear Goals

Establishing norms—collective commitments—is a great first step for teams, but it's important to translate those good intentions into results. Begin by examining data to determine the greatest area of need in student learning, and then set clear and measurable targets for improvements in those areas. In PLCs, these targets are expressed as *goals*—"measurable milestones that can be used to assess progress in advancing toward a vision" (DuFour et al., 2010b, p. 3). Specifically, these goals are SMART—specific, measurable, attainable, results oriented, and time bound (O'Neill & Conzemius, 2006). These goals are not focused on what we, as educators, do. Rather, they are focused on what students will do as a result of the team's actions. They target critical areas for improvement in student learning, and therefore are designed to not only guide focused improvement but also provide a process for monitoring progress toward their attainment—the results.

The most powerful part of the process, however, is the development and implementation of an action plan that is designed to close the gap between the current reality and the goal. The plan may include a number of actions and steps that focus on closing that gap, ranging from curriculum alignment, the use of formative assessments, implementation of effective instructional practices, and targeted interventions. The SMART Goals and Action Planning Worksheet (page 100 in the Tools for Teams appendix) shows the process teams can follow to establish SMART goals and design action plans that take these critical areas into consideration.

Celebrate Success

Working as a collaborative team is certainly rewarding, but it can definitely be hard work. Be sure to keep perspective and maintain momentum by celebrating along the way. Use gains in student achievement and other team accomplishments as sources of inspiration. Schedule celebrations into your meeting agendas so that you won't forget to take time to recognize the results your team has achieved.

Full Speed Ahead

We hope this chapter has helped you recharge your knowledge about PLCs and affirmed or even refined your understanding about how your team can function more effectively. Ensuring your team's ability to function effectively and efficiently establishes a strong foundation and framework within which you can tackle the challenges and embrace the rewards of what we consider to be one of the most pivotal and exciting parts of being a PLC—creating and using common formative assessments. The next chapter will frame the overall topic of assessment and set the stage for starting the process.

CHAPTER 2

Setting the Stage for Common Formative Assessments

KEY POINTS

- There is compelling research that says that frequent formative assessments improve student achievement for all students.
- Common formative assessments do not have to be tests or quizzes.
- Common formative assessments do not have to take a long time to administer or include lengthy student work products.
- If you don't use the results of the common formative assessment to make a difference in student learning, the assessment is summative.

As we discussed in chapter 1, four critical questions guide the work of teams in PLCs (DuFour et al., 2010a, p. 28):

1. What knowledge and skills should every student acquire as a result of this unit of instruction?

2. How will we know when each student has acquired the essential knowledge and skills?

3. How will we respond when some students do not learn?

4. How will we extend and enrich the learning for students who are already proficient?

This book will help your team confidently answer the second question by using common formative assessments. Specifically, this chapter will help define what common formative assessments are and how they fit into a well-developed, balanced assessment system.

When your team begins to create assessments to determine whether or not students have learned the identified essential learning outcomes, you are beginning the work that many believe is pivotal to the process—the work that will really make a difference for your students, but that will also challenge you as a teacher. Before teachers really understand this work, we often hear them say, "We are already testing kids too much. Why would we want to do more testing?" and "I already know which of my kids need help. I don't need another test to tell me that." These teachers aren't being difficult; they are just expressing their concern that any instructional time they take away from the teaching process will have a negative impact on their students.

Once teachers begin this work and start to see success, they understand that writing and using common formative assessments is not *one more thing* but rather an integral part of the teaching and learning process. Let's examine what teams need to know to help them see the value of this important step in the PLC process.

Formative Versus Summative Assessment

Most teachers are comfortable that they know the difference between formative and summative assessments. They know that formative assessments are assessments *for* learning and summative assessments are assessments *of* learning (Stiggins, Arter, Chappuis, & Chappuis, 2004).

Other assessment experts have written about the difference. For example, according to Reeves (2009):

> It is absolutely vital that we understand the true meaning of formative assessments— an activity designed to give meaningful feedback to students and teachers and to improve professional practice and student achievement. Tests designed only to render an evaluation cannot achieve the potential of assessment for learning that assessment experts have suggested is an essential element of effective practice. (p. 91)

DuFour, Eaker, and Karhanek (2010) clarify formative assessments even further:

> Three things must occur for the assessment to be formative: (1) the assessment is used to identify students who are experiencing difficulty, (2) those students are provided additional time and support to acquire the intended skill or concept, and (3) the students are given another opportunity to demonstrate that they've learned. (p. 63)

We address this clarification in more detail throughout this book. Chapter 7 will help teams see how to use the results from these assessments to identify not only *which* students need help but also *what kind of help* they need. In that chapter, we also explore ways that teams can find the time to provide help for identified students. Later in the chapter, we also explore the idea of how teams will need to think differently about their grading practices once they begin using formative assessments.

We believe the purpose of the assessment and how teams use the results is what really determines whether it is formative or summative, not how it's written or administered. If the assessment occurs during the learning process, and the results will be used to help students continue to learn, it is considered formative. As DuFour et al. (2010b) note, *formative assessment* is "used to advance and not merely monitor each student's learning; the assessment informs the teacher regarding the effectiveness of instruction and the individual student regarding progress in becoming proficient" (p. 3). If the assessment occurs after the learning is complete, and is used to give a grade or provide a final measure of student results, it is *summative*. So the biggest difference will not be in what the assessment looks like but rather in how teachers respond to the results. For example, if an English teacher asks her students to complete a graphic organizer comparing themes of two stories, grades the assignment, and then returns them to her students believing it's a formative assessment, she's confused the difference between formative and summative. What would make this assessment formative is if she used the assignment to determine which of her students were not able to compare the themes of the stories and then provided them with additional instruction as a result of the information.

You will learn in chapters 4 and 5 that in order to develop truly effective formative assessments, you will need to break *standards*—the narrowest item listed by a state when describing what students should know and be able to do—into each of the learning targets that are made clear to students. *Learning targets* are the smaller skills, strategies, and pieces of content information a student needs to know in order to be able to complete the standard (see figure 2.1). The process your team will use to carefully uncover these learning targets is described in chapter 4, The Unwrapping Process: Achieving Collective Clarity on Learning Targets.

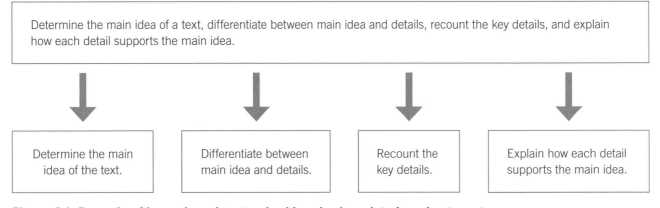

Figure 2.1: Example of how a learning standard breaks down into learning targets.

The term *standard* is used throughout this chapter in a generic way. The Common Core State Standards Initiative uses the term *standard* to "define the knowledge and skills students should have within their K–12 education careers so that they will graduate high school able to succeed in entry-level, credit-bearing academic college courses and in workforce training programs" (Common Core State Standards Initiative, 2010a). However, before these standards were developed, most states used a variety of terminology to mean this same thing. For example, Arizona uses the term *performance objective*, and Illinois uses the term *performance descriptor*. And to make it even more complicated for teachers, even within the same state, standards often are written with a different *grain size*. That is, one might be a specific skill, while another, a much larger learning outcome.

This concept of unwrapping is one of the key strategies teams can use to write formative assessments to guide their instruction. A formative assessment is usually written around learning targets (specific skills and strategies), and a summative assessment is usually written around more complex standards or even multiple standards. The reason that this is important is that the learning targets are the step-by-step processes we teach students as they move toward their understanding of a bigger concept. We assess them formatively so that we know exactly how to respond when a student is experiencing difficulty during the learning process.

In chapter 5, your team will learn a process for designing a formative assessment around a small number of learning targets so that you can identify and respond to students who haven't learned the targets in an expeditious way.

Some common misconceptions many teams have about formative assessments are that they have to be written, they have to be tests or quizzes, or they have to be lengthy. Formative assessments can be student work samples and activities previously used by teachers as practice during the unit of instruction. They can also be performances teachers watch and score against a rubric. Effective formative assessments are intentionally short in terms of the number of questions or items, and they should take only a short time for students to complete. Because we want teams to feel like their assessment practices are a seamless part of teaching and learning, and because we want them to occur frequently, it is important that they be short enough in length that they don't interrupt the instructional process. We encourage teachers to design assessments that take as few as fifteen to twenty minutes to administer.

What Does *Common* Mean?

The term *common assessment* refers to those assessments given by teacher teams who teach the same content or grade level—those with "collective responsibility for the learning of a group of students who are expected to acquire the same knowledge and skills" (DuFour et al., 2010b, p. 2). For the assessment to be common, no teacher can opt out of the process; it must be common to all teachers who teach that course or grade level. DuFour et al. (2010b) add that common assessments use "the same instrument or a common process utilizing the same criteria for determining the quality of student work" (p. 2). This means that if a rubric is used, the teachers must work on building not only a common understanding of what the rubric means but also use collaborative scoring practices to ensure the results are the same no matter which teacher applied the rubric.

Benefits of Common Assessments

The benefits of common formative assessments are great. DuFour et al. (2010a, p. 80) state that common formative assessments do the following:

- Promote efficiency for teachers
- Promote equity for students
- Provide an effective strategy for determining whether the guaranteed curriculum is being taught and, more importantly, learned
- Inform the practice of individual teachers
- Build a team's capacity to improve its program
- Facilitate a systematic, collective response to student who are experiencing difficulty
- Offer the most powerful tool for changing adult behavior and practice

Some teachers are concerned that collaborating to do this work will take away from the time they have to prepare for their classrooms. However, when considering the amount of time each teacher currently puts into the assessment process, doing the work collaboratively should result in more efficient work. Rather than starting from scratch, many teams begin the process by sharing their current assessments and choosing those ideas and items that appear to be most effective. Your team will likely experience a shift in how you work together as you move from *sharing* your current practice to actually building assessments together. Teams that design common formative assessments have more in-depth discussions about proficiency and, as they analyze the resulting data, have more focused conversations about instructional strategies (Graham & Ferriter, 2008).

One of the principles of PLCs is that teams engage in collective inquiry—that they learn together. They build shared knowledge around best practices so that they increase student learning (DuFour et al., 2008). Consider how your team will learn together as you write and use formative assessments. You will likely become better assessment designers and will strengthen your skills in analyzing and using data.

While analyzing data, your team will share instructional strategies and determine if some of those strategies are more effective than others. Even if there is no one strategy that works best, you will have an opportunity to add to your repertoire of strategies so that you can respond in a different way to the students who didn't learn it the first time.

When your team works to answer question one—What knowledge and skills should every student acquire as a result of this unit of instruction?—you begin the process of assuring equity for all of the students your team serves. In chapter 3, we'll lay out a process that teams use to build consensus about how to answer this first important question. This guaranteed and viable curriculum (Marzano, 2003) becomes the focus for your formative assessments.

Equity means that your students will learn the same important learning targets no matter which teacher they have. While this concept sounds good for students, it also has an important benefit for teachers. That is, when students are commonly prepared for the next course or grade level, as happens when they get equitable content, the next teacher doesn't have to use valuable instructional time filling in content for some students so that all students have the same prerequisite skills and information. Common formative assessments help ensure equity because they are written around agreed-on learning targets. One of the important steps your team will take while developing these assessments is to discuss what proficiency will look like. Coming to consensus about proficiency is critical for guaranteeing equity for your students.

In addition, your team will have a greater capacity to respond when students need more time and support. DuFour et al. (2010a) argue that when students experience difficulty learning, members of collaborative teams must provide additional time and support through an intervention system that is timely, directive, and systematic. They describe many examples of systematic interventions that effectively meet these characteristics. Interventions may range from differentiated instructional strategies, smaller grouping to monitor incomplete work, and even enrichment opportunities, to name a few. For example, after analyzing the results of their common formative assessments, teams may move students from one classroom into another *for a short time* to provide specific and targeted learning support. If there are three classes on the team, each teacher takes one group of students for response. One teacher takes all of the students who need more time and support with an opportunity for teaching the target using an alternate instructional strategy, another takes the students who need additional practice, and the third teacher takes those who could benefit from enrichment.

When talking about intervention, we use the term *corrective instruction* to describe strategies teams can use to respond to the results of their common formative assessments. *Corrective instruction* is instruction that occurs for some students whose assessment results indicate they have not learned a particular skill or strategy at a proficient level. It is instruction that is *different* than the initial instruction in a way that teachers believe will help the student understand and learn the skill or strategy.

The response to intervention (RTI) model is built on the premise that not all students learn the same way and at the same speed. PLCs build a system of responses to assure students will be provided the time and the instructional strategies they need to be successful. They embrace formative assessment as a way to identify which students need additional support and which students need extension or enrichment. Therefore, after initial instruction, the team administers a common formative assessment to identify which students require corrective instruction. These students are then provided with the necessary help. For some students, this initial extra support still won't be enough. Teams monitor students by using additional progress monitoring to identify which students need even more support.

Finally, your team will benefit from the professional learning that takes place as you talk in more detail after the assessment about effective instructional strategies, effective assessment strategies, and effective ways to respond to students.

As we have described, common assessments can be either formative or summative depending on their purpose. A common summative assessment, for example, might be a final exam that the entire biology team uses at the end of the year in high school. Remember that these are considered summative *because* they occur at the end of the learning and their purpose is *merely* to give a grade. In chapter 7, we'll explore ways that teams could use the results of their tests *at the end of each unit* in a formative way to provide even more time and support for the students who still haven't learned it after initial instruction.

Putting It Together

PLCs focus on common formative assessments for their work together because of the compelling research that these are the assessments that can truly improve student achievement.

In their meta-analysis on classroom assessment, Black and Wiliam (1998) report a 0.4 to 0.7 standard deviation increase in student achievement with the use of frequent formative assessment. This research was conducted for all grade and age levels. The most improvement was seen for the lowest-achieving students. Wiliam (2007) follows up by saying, "When implemented well, formative assessment can effectively double the speed of student learning" (pp. 36–37).

Popham (2006) explains it is important that this research not be misinterpreted to mean that any kind of testing will provide similar results:

> Educators need to realize that the research rationale for formative assessments is based on short cycle assessments. Such rapid-turnaround assessments yield results during a class period or in the midst of a multiweek instructional unit. If the results don't get back in time for teachers to adjust instruction for the students being assessed, then it's not formative assessment. (p. 86)

Finally, as Wiggins (2006) so eloquently reminds us: "The more you teach without finding out who understands the information and who doesn't, the greater the likelihood that only already-proficient students will succeed." If we *don't* use formative assessment, we are basically regressing back to the "I taught it, they just didn't learn it" mentality. And in the end, the students who need it the most will lose out.

A Balanced Assessment System

Because of the strong research base for using formative assessments, schools are successfully creating these team-based assessments in addition to a variety of other types of assessments. They want to have all the necessary information they need about their students. Therefore, they recognize the importance of a balanced assessment system.

In a balanced assessment system, teachers have access to both formative and summative information in order to make short- and long-term decisions to help their students. So what does a balanced assessment system look like, and why do we need each type of assessment?

Table 2.1 shows the pieces of a balanced assessment system. They include classroom assessments, common formative assessments, interim or benchmark assessments, and external summative assessments. (This Balanced Assessment System Framework also appears on page 101 of the Tools for Teams appendix.)

Table 2.1: A Balanced Assessment System

	Classroom Assessments		Common Formative Assessments	Interim or Benchmark Assessments	External Summative Assessments
Examples of practice	Worksheets, clickers, whiteboards, exit slips, conferences	Final exams, final projects	Tasks assessed with rubrics, short quizzes, common worksheets, and clickers	Quarterly tests or performances, writing samples	State tests, and ACT, SAT, and Advanced Placement (AP) exams
Formative or summative?	Very formative	More summative	Very formative	More summative	Summative
Whose responsibility?	Classroom teachers	Classroom teachers	Collaborative teams at each school	District teams of representative teachers	An external group of "experts"
Purpose?	To give immediate feedback	To give a grade	To determine if students have learned the material and how to responding	To assess curriculum, instructional strategies, and pacing	To determine whether curriculum, instructional strategies, and pacing were appropriate

Classroom Assessments

First, there is nothing about common formative assessment that precludes teachers from using their own classroom assessments in addition to common team-developed assessments. In fact, we encourage teachers to use a variety of strategies to gather immediate feedback during each lesson about whether students understand the concepts being taught. Good instructional practices that provide immediate information include checking for understanding with questions; monitoring students as they work independently and in groups to provide feedback and support; using clickers (each student has a device connected to a hardware system that he or she uses to respond to questions so the teacher can see who responded, in what way, and how many students were correct or incorrect), whiteboards, and exit slips (or "tickets out the door") that ask a few questions about the lesson; as well as administering teacher-created quizzes. Whenever teachers engage their students in practices that provide the teacher (as well as students) with information about whether they have successfully learned a target, the practice is considered an assessment. For example, if teachers ask their students to respond to the question, "What is the difference between a plant and animal cell?" as an exit slip, they can easily sort the responses into groups of who did or did not learn the difference. Because the teacher knows *by student* who needs more time, the practice is considered a formative assessment. Thus, classroom formative assessments are still necessary in the work of PLCs.

Summative assessments happen at the end of the learning process and are used to give grades. In addition, because formative assessments are often written around more isolated learning targets, summative assessments are intended to make sure that students can put skills and strategies together to be able to accomplish what we typically call the *standards of learning*. For example, a science department may have an overall goal that students can design and carry out an experiment following the scientific method to gather good information to prove a hypothesis. Teachers may create a number of formative assessments around specific learning targets: Can the student create a hypothesis? Does the student know a number of different ways to gather and arrange data? Can the student use correct safety procedures in the lab? The summative assessment, however, requires the student to be able to put all of these skills together to answer a specific scientific question.

Consider, for example, the following standard from the sixth- through eighth-grade writing standards for literacy in history/social studies, science, and technical subjects 6–12 from the Common Core State Standards (Common Core State Standards Initiative, 2010b):

> Conduct short research projects to answer a question (including a self-generated question), drawing on several sources and generating additional related, focused questions that allow for multiple avenues of exploration. (p. 66)

The team might identify the following skills as important skills for students to know and be able to do in order to accomplish this standard: locate multiple sources of information about a specific topic, develop research questions to ask about a topic, and even evaluate the adequacy of the amount and type of information gathered about the topic to determine if the information is sufficient. The team could create formative assessments around one or more of these specific learning targets. However, it's possible that a student could carry out each of these learning targets and still not be able to conduct a quality research project as required in the standard. Thus, good assessment practice requires both short formative assessments around specific learning targets and final summative assessment around the learning standard.

We believe that until a student has mastered the essential outcomes being taught in a unit of instruction, there must be additional support beyond the core instruction. The core instruction includes initial classroom teaching, formative assessment around identified learning targets, and intervention—corrective instruction or extensions—around those learning targets. When the summative assessment identifies students who are not yet proficient, then the student is provided Tier 2 support for further learning. In this case, the student might be pulled out for additional small group instruction during a time where no direct instruction is occurring in the classroom. For example, a student who is still experiencing difficulty writing a coherent paragraph after the class is finished with that unit is provided specific targeted intervention on that skill. In another example, a high school algebra student who is still having difficulty understanding how to solve a quadratic equation after the unit is completed would get help in a resource class during her study hall until she demonstrates that she understands this concept. This is not to say that instruction waits. The students who need additional support continue moving forward with the next unit along with their classmates. However, concurrently, they are receiving support in the crucial skills and concepts that are essential.

Common Formative Assessments

Common formative assessments, the assessments your team will develop and use to assure students are learning and to know what to do next when they need additional time and support, are the focus of your work as a team and the purpose of this book.

Common formative assessments are written by teacher teams around the learning targets the team has identified as the most important ones to be taught. They help your team know not only which students have learned the targets but also what to do for the students who have not. They do not have to be pencil-and-paper tests or quizzes; they can be individual student work samples, completed graphic organizers, writing pieces, products, or performances. They are written around a small number of learning targets, and therefore are not intended to take a long time to administer. Ideally, they can be scored quickly so that the team can respond in a timely fashion when it identifies students experiencing difficulty.

Consider, for example, the seventh-grade English team that is working on the following standard from the Common Core State Standards: "Support claim(s) with logical reasoning and relevant evidence, using accurate, credible sources and demonstrating an understanding of the topic or text" (Common Core State Standards Initiative, 2010b, p. 42). First, team members identify the student-friendly learning target: "I can support my position by providing evidence." Then they give their students the statement "Video games are harmful to adolescents" and ask them to take one side of the issue and find evidence to support their position. Their short formative assessment is for students to write one paragraph laying out their position and backing it up with support.

One important characteristic of common formative assessments is that any constructed-response questions or performance targets are assessed using a common rubric developed for that assessment. The team of teachers agrees on the rubric and practices collaborative scoring so that all of the team members are using the rubric in the same way. Throughout this book, we'll discuss how to design and use rubrics to provide feedback to students.

Benchmark Assessments

Many schools and districts are creating *benchmark assessments* given periodically to determine whether their students are making progress toward the mastery of standards.

It's important to note that some benchmarks are designed to monitor student attainment of specific standards that have been addressed through classroom instruction prior to its administration. Often, they are designed in alignment to a specific pacing guide. For example, the district may decide that all schools will teach five standards during the first quarter in a particular subject area. The district then creates a summative assessment to be given at the end of that quarter. Other benchmark assessments are designed more globally to monitor student growth along a recursive set of standards, some of which may not have been addressed during instruction. If your school or district is using benchmark assessments, it's critical to understand how they are structured and the purpose for their implementation.

Larry Ainsworth (2006) suggests that benchmark assessments have two benefits. The first is that they have "predictive value" for how students will do on the next level of assessment (the state test). They also help the team plan for future instruction and assessment. If the benchmark assessment is written in the same style as the state assessment or other external summative assessment (like an AP exam), students have an opportunity, before the end of the year, to practice the type of assessment item as well as know where they are on the path toward mastering each of the standards.

External Summative Assessments

Almost all of us are required to administer state assessments toward the end of the year. The purpose of these tests is to determine what percentage of our students fell into each of several levels: below proficiency, at proficiency, and exceeds proficiency. Teachers generally view these as high-stakes tests because the results are reported and publicized, often comparing school to school within a state or city. These tests are used to determine whether a school is making AYP (adequate yearly progress) toward all students being proficient. Schools that are not making AYP are often given sanctions or penalties. Other external summative assessments many schools use include AP exams, the SAT, the ACT, and achievement tests.

In a PLC, teachers believe that it is their responsibility to ensure that all kids learn. State assessments provide a common understanding of what that learning must look like for all kids. Schools use the results of this yearly assessment to determine their current reality, identify their greatest area of need (O'Neill & Conzemius, 2006), and set SMART goals for the year.

Finding the Balance

Each of these assessments is necessary for teams to create a balanced view of student learning. Teachers want to know, as they are teaching a concept, whether or not students are understanding, and they use classroom formative assessment strategies to gather that kind of feedback. Team-developed common formative assessments help teams of teachers respond—*during* the learning process—to students who need more time and support as well as those who could benefit from enrichment strategies. The team capitalizes on the benefits of collaboration to use the best strategies for instruction and corrective instruction. Periodic benchmark assessments provide checks during the school year to assure that students are making progress on proficiency toward the standards to be assessed at the end of the year on high-stakes tests. External summative assessments help schools and districts remain accountable for all students in their schools.

As teams begin the process of developing common formative assessments, they should look at their list of current assessments, considering whether they have appropriate assessments in each category and whether they have some current assessments that overlap in purpose. If so, any redundant assessments could be discontinued to provide more time for teams to work on common formative assessments. Sometimes teams will discover that they have a plethora of summative and external assessments already in place, but don't have adequate formative assessments. In this case, they should discuss the possibility of eliminating some of their summative assessments.

In many districts, there are required assessments teachers must use. Early in the development of common formative assessments, teams may find that they are doing duplicate work because their districts still require them to administer everything on the original assessment list. If this is the case for your team, you may want to keep a list of all the assessments administered over a quarter of the school year and note the amount of student contact time it takes to administer them. This data can help you understand whether or not there really is too much time being given to assessment and whether there really is too much overlap of information. Our experience has been that sometimes duplicate summative assessments can be eliminated once administrators, teachers, and parents are confident that the common formative assessments are more beneficial, particularly when the summative assessments provide redundant information.

Do We Have Time to Do It All?

Your team may be worried about the amount of time it will take to create, administer, analyze, and respond to common formative assessments—most teams are. But many teams are already successfully doing this work and feel confident that the time they are spending is worth it. So how do they make it work?

First, we believe that teams need to have time during the contractual school day to do the work of PLCs (DuFour et al., 2010a). Once teachers learn about the compelling research behind formative assessments, they are invested in the process. The PLC model supports teacher learning, and teams that write and administer these assessments are doing some of the most powerful professional development they can do. Much of the work your team will engage in is like the work each individual teacher has done in the past. The difference is that, by doing it together, teachers benefit from the insights of the group instead of relying on only their own knowledge.

As teams get started in the process, they generally find that the steps might initially take longer than they will once the team becomes more assessment literate and has experienced a full cycle of design, implementation, analysis, and action. It's good to recognize, however, that teams that use common formative assessments on a regular basis become so familiar with the process that they can accomplish much more and their product is much better than when they first started.

For example, when starting out, teams may need a full meeting to discuss which targets of learning they will assess and when they will administer the assessment. They will likely use another meeting to write the actual assessment and discuss proficiency. Once they've administered the assessment, it will probably take an additional meeting to analyze the data and develop the plan for responding to student needs. Teams that work on this over a period of several years find that they are able to expedite the process, focusing more on the revision of assessments instead of developing new assessments. In chapter 1, we talked about how teams create a work flow from meeting to meeting. Using one meeting to write common formative assessments and the next meeting to analyze the results and plan the response is an example of how this work flow looks.

Grading Practices

When your team begins to develop and use common formative assessments, it won't be long before someone will ask, "If these assessments are being given *during the learning process,* should they be graded?" The easy answer is that they should not be graded. As O'Connor (2007) states:

> Grades are broken if scores for everything students do find their way into report card grades. The fix is to include, in all but specific, limited cases, only evidence from summative

assessments intended to document learning, that is, designed to serve as assessments *of* learning. (p. 95)

Teachers might be concerned that if they don't grade an assignment or assessment, students won't be motivated to do their best work. However, the research clearly suggests that this is not the case. Actually, research has shown that when a grade is given, the student does *not* learn how to do better from that evaluation. In a study conducted about the motivation value of grades and feedback, one group of students was given only grades for a task, one group comments only, and one group grades plus comments. Researchers then measured students' performance on subsequent tasks. Students who were given only comments had significantly greater improvement than those given only grades or those who received both grades and comments (Butler, 1988). Corrective feedback seems to hold the power for improved learning.

Another concern some teachers have about not grading common formative assessments is that they won't have scores in their gradebook to effectively grade students at the end of the grading period. When schools use a standards-based report card, teachers can easily collect common formative assessments as evidence of the body of student work they are using to determine where the student is currently in the learning process. However, teachers in districts with a more traditional reporting system will find it hard to know what to do with the scores on these assessments. O'Connor (2007) suggests that teachers keep two parts to their gradebook—one with formative results and another with summative results. The final grade is computed using only summative scores, but the formative scores allow students and their parents to know where the students' learning is throughout the quarter.

Rick DuFour advocates a process that considers both of these teacher concerns. He suggests that collaborative teams grade the initial assessment, identifying the students who need additional time and support for learning. Then the team or school must provide the specific intervention students need to become proficient. Once a student has shown proficiency, the grade on the initial assessment is changed to reflect the new learning (DuFour, 2010).

Changing the grading system is a significant endeavor in any school or district. O'Connor (2007) calls grades "the last frontier" (p. 127). We agree with this statement and recommend that schools wait to discuss changing the grading system until the need for change emerges naturally. In other words, after teams have been working with common formative assessments for a period of time, they will have evidence of why a traditional grading system doesn't really accurately tell parents what students have learned. A revised grading system serves no purpose until you have a more accurate way to collect evidence of what students actually have learned. Teams will learn more from writing and using common formative assessments than from planning to change the grading system.

Gathering and Collecting Data

As teams increase their use of common formative assessments, they may find it beneficial to explore the idea of how to use technology to gather, sort, and store this information. We have worked with teams that use spreadsheet programs to gather and sort their data. They meet in a room with a projector and sort the data for each learning target as they discuss the results and next steps. Other schools and districts have purchased technology specifically for this use. One school district, for example, has a scanner and printer at each school so that teachers can run student answer sheets through the scanner and get a printout of the results by student and learning target. The software program aggregates (adds up) all the results for individual teachers and prints out the data totals (see chapter 7 for what data to look for) that teachers can use to make decisions about next steps.

Before investing in expensive equipment and software, however, teams should develop and use the results of a variety of common formative assessments to determine if a software program will help them. Depending on the frequency of assessment, the types of assessment, and the number of teachers and students involved, some teams prefer to rely on their own tools to gather data and make decisions. These tools might include data tables they personally design or even Excel spreadsheets that are used to sort data they enter from each assessment. In chapter 3, we help teams begin the work of developing common formative assessments by helping them see how to answer the first critical question, What is it we want students to know and be able to do? This work becomes the foundation for the rest of the assessment process.

CHAPTER 3

Power Standards—
The Essential Outcomes

KEY POINTS

- We monitor what we value. Teams must agree about what is most important for their students to learn and what it will look like when students learn it.

- All standards are not equal in value.

- Teams can use a process to identify the most important outcomes they have for their students.

- Power standards are the basis for common formative assessments and for determining the additional time and support students need when they experience difficulty.

The purpose of this book is to provide a toolkit for teams to use to write common formative assessments to monitor the learning of their students. The first step in the process is for teams to decide *what* they are going to assess. They need to be clear on the skills, concepts, and processes that students must know in a course or grade in order to be successful both now and in future classes or grade levels. In this chapter, we discuss how teams can reach consensus about this important information.

First, let's explore why it is important to spend team time before you begin writing assessments to determine which of your course or grade-level standards are most essential to teach.

Almost every teacher we talk to shares a concern that he or she has too much to teach. Most teachers have had the experience of trying to cover their curriculum and then realizing at some point during the school year they won't be able to accomplish everything. They are faced with the decision to leave out content or to rush through what's left on the list, hoping to give their students enough background information so that they will be successful on the end-of-year test. This happens because we really do have too much to teach. Marzano and Kendall (1998) examined the list of national standards and determined how long it would take to teach each standard. When they looked at the actual amount of teaching time most schools have, they concluded that it would take about twenty-three years to teach the entire list of national standards. Since no school districts have this amount of time, each individual classroom teacher must make decisions about what to include on his or her must-teach list.

When each teacher must make these decisions independently, schools face what Schmoker and Marzano (1999) call "curriculum chaos." Some teachers choose a favorite unit, others might teach what they believe will most likely be on the state test, and still others choose from what the textbook emphasizes. Because teachers make these decisions independently, their students receive a different curriculum—even though all the teachers believe they are teaching the same standards.

Moving From Individual to Team Decisions

When teams begin to work together within PLCs, the first question they generally work to answer is, What do we want our students to know and be able to do? Team members are often surprised to find that their colleagues may be emphasizing standards that are different from the ones they're emphasizing.

Most people believe that having a common set of state standards ensures that all students are learning the same curriculum. Some schools and districts try to assure this common curriculum by mapping the curriculum so that all teachers are teaching the same standard at the same time. While this does help teams develop a more common understanding of the curriculum, it certainly doesn't result in a *guaranteed and viable curriculum* (Marzano, 2003). In his book *What Works in Schools*, Marzano (2003) identifies the most important factors successful schools have in place. The number-one factor is a guaranteed and viable curriculum. He explains that the term *guaranteed* means that any student in the school will be taught the same content and to the same degree of understanding. He also says, though, that the curriculum must be *viable*. By this, he means that teachers have adequate time to teach the curriculum. Yet even when given a list of the state standards, curriculum documents, and a curriculum map, teachers still interpret the standards in many different ways.

Consider what happens, for example, when a fifth-grade team of three teachers in a traditional school looks at the list of Common Core English language arts standards for its students in the area of informative or explanatory text. The teachers look at the following standards:

> Write informative/explanatory texts to examine a topic and convey ideas and information clearly.
>
> a. Introduce a topic clearly, provide a general observation and focus, and group related information logically; include formatting (e.g., headings), illustrations, and multimedia when useful to aiding comprehension.
>
> b. Develop the topic with facts, definitions, concrete details, quotations, or other information and examples related to the topic.
>
> c. Link ideas within and across categories of information using words, phrases, and clauses (e.g., *in contrast, especially*).
>
> d. Use precise language and domain-specific vocabulary to inform about or explain the topic.
>
> e. Provide a concluding statement or section related to the information or explanation presented. (Common Core State Standards Initiative, 2010b, p. 20)

If the team doesn't build consensus about what understanding will look like for its students, individual teachers could teach to distinctly different understandings. One teacher could easily emphasize the structure of writing, asking her students to work on topic sentences, supporting details, and conclusions using a graphic organizer to help students see the link between the introduction and the conclusion and the need for support in between. A second teacher on this team could emphasize the development of ideas in writing, helping her students support their topic sentences with examples, elaborations, and explanations. Her graphic organizer could provide an outline form for students to use to build the structure of their piece of writing. The third teacher on the team could emphasize the development of word choice and transitions between sentences by focusing on teaching students how to add interest and depth to their writing. Each of these teachers would be able to say that he or she was teaching the standards laid out for fifth graders. When these students move on to sixth grade, they will likely be prepared for sixth-grade writing. However, they will all be prepared *differently*. The sixth-grade teacher will have to spend some amount of time filling in the gaps for each of her students, rather than being able to build on the common preparation of all of her students.

Imagine, instead, if these three teachers wrestled with the difficult work of deciding what they believed fifth-grade writing should look like. They would determine what to emphasize, what students should master, and what mastery would look like. They would decide which standards to assess frequently and formatively, and when to provide more time and support for students experiencing difficulty. For example, in the fifth-grade writing example, teachers might agree that all fifth graders must be able to write a strong introduction and conclusion. They would likely develop a rubric indicating what an effective introduction and conclusion look like. These concepts would be taught and common formative assessments used to determine whether students achieved proficiency. Students who can't write an introduction and a conclusion would get additional instruction specific to their needs and be reassessed to assure mastery.

Defining *Most Important*

If we asked a team to work together to establish a list of most-important outcomes of learning, it is likely each team member would have a different view about what makes one standard more important than another. A teacher's experience, philosophy, and personal interests often affect his or her perspective about priorities. In fact, Reeves (2002) describes a process he uses with teams to get them thinking about what they really believe is important. He asks them to consider what they would tell a new teacher teaching the grade or course before theirs who inquired about the most important things students should know before advancing to the next grade. This reflection gets teachers thinking about the fact that they instinctively prioritize what they are teaching despite the fact they never really realized they were prioritizing or making decisions about what they personally consider most important. Once they realize that they are, in fact, making these decisions, they see how important it is to build consensus with the other people teaching this course or grade level so that students have the same expected outcomes.

We recommend that teams begin with some reflection about their individual priorities—perhaps by asking themselves the question Reeves (2002) suggests. Once each teacher has worked independently to create their list of most importants, the team should share and compare its ideas to understand how close, or how different, members' lists are. Teams learn a lot from this discussion about their current reality, but they must still build consensus about the most-important outcomes.

Power Standards

The real work of defining what is most important for your students to know and be able to do will come as a result of identifying *essential learning*—"the critical skills, knowledge, and dispositions each student must acquire as a result of each course, grade level, and unit of instruction" (DuFour et al., 2010b,

p. 3)—what Reeves (2002) calls *power standards*. He suggests that teams identify—from their current state standards—those that are the most important for all students to know using a process laid out by his colleague Larry Ainsworth (2004).

Teachers will still teach all of the standards, but they will emphasize the power standards in their work. We believe teams that identify these most important power standards can use them as the foundation of their assessment work. That is, these are the standards they will unwrap and use to identify learning targets (as we describe in chapter 4). Then teams write their common formative assessments around these standards and use them to gauge the need for additional time and support with interventions when students experience difficulty. These assessments become the foundation of the work teams do together.

Achieving Clarity About Standards Vocabulary

As this book is being written, many states have agreed to adopt the Common Core State Standards, but most are still using their own standards during this time of transition. The Common Core State Standards are written for mathematics and English language arts for all grades K–12 and build from grade level to grade level.

As it stands, each state has developed its own vocabulary to describe the parts of the curriculum included in its own standards documents, and the standards vary widely from state to state. Additionally, most states use the term *standard* to mean something different. For our purposes, *standard* means the narrowest item listed by a state when describing what students should know and be able to do. For example, in West Virginia these are called *objectives*; in Illinois they're called *performance descriptors*. As we mentioned in chapter 2, even in the same state these statements may have a different "grain size"; that is, the statement may be very specific or very general in what is expected for students. For example, in the Illinois science standards, students are asked to "Describe the relationships among organisms in their environment" as well as "Formulate questions on a specific science topic and choose the steps needed to answer the questions." The first standard is fairly narrow in scope and fairly specific in the knowledge and skills students will need to know. The second standard is a broader process and will likely take more time and incorporate more knowledge and skills to accomplish. Thus, it has a larger grain size. The new Common Core State Standards minimize this variation, and most standards are now written at a similar grain size.

What Makes Learning *Essential*?

Reeves (2002) suggests three criteria to determine whether or not a standard is a power standard: endurance, leverage, and readiness for the next level of learning. Endurance defines something a student will need to know for a longer period of time—certainly beyond preparation for a test. These are standards that are used during subsequent units of instruction and over a period of years. For example, when students learn how to use context clues to understand the meaning of unknown words, they use that skill for the rest of their lives. The second criterion is leverage. This means that the standard is taught and used in more than one curricular area. Sometimes we call this a "bang for your buck" standard. For example, students are taught how to read graphs in math and apply this skill in science. Sometimes states even have the same or similar standard in two different curricular areas. The third criterion is readiness for the next level of learning. Some standards are taught because they are prerequisite skills for future learning. For example, logarithms are taught in math because students will need to know how to use and interpret them in higher-level classes such as college chemistry. In kindergarten, students are taught letter-sound recognition because it is a prerequisite skill to learn to read. To determine if a standard is a power standard, teachers apply these three criteria. If a standard has one or more of these characteristics, it is considered a power standard. Ainsworth (2004) suggests that teams look for approximately one-third of their state standards to fit one or more of these criteria.

Building Consensus as a Team

Larry Ainsworth (2004) has laid out a process for identifying power standards that accounts for both individual interpretation as well as building a collaborative understanding. He recommends that teams consider both.

First, teachers individually review the list of standards for a subject area. We recommend that all teachers meet to do this step together even though they will be working independently at the beginning. By meeting together, you will assure that everyone takes about the same amount of time to complete the process. This is important because this step shouldn't take a great deal of time. This initial identification should be almost a gut decision—if teachers spend too much time thinking about the criteria, they will eventually decide that each of their standards fit one or more of the criteria! Instead, each teacher reads through the list of standards and marks those that he or she believes are the power standards—those standards that fit one of the three criteria of endurance, leverage, and readiness for the next level of learning. Some standards will fit more than one of these criteria. Of course, during this first step, all teachers are unlikely to pick out the exact same standards to be the power standards.

In the next step, teachers will need to come to agreement. The second step is to build consensus as a team about which standards are power standards (Ainsworth, 2004). During this step, it is important for everyone to have a voice in the outcome. Some teams will use a more formal process than others to develop consensus, but the important point is that the final product needs to be agreed on by everyone. It is important that during this process the teams build consensus rather than just voting or looking for those standards that the majority has identified. This process might take some time as teachers will want to explain their reasoning—whether they included it or not—so that the team members can weigh all of their ideas and viewpoints. During this discussion, the team is also getting more clarity and agreement about what the standards mean.

For example, some teams start their work by going through the list of standards to see if there are any that *everyone* agrees are power standards or that *no one* agrees are power standards. Then they begin to work through the rest of the standards one at a time, talking about who marked or didn't mark each as a power standard and why. Teachers discuss what they think the standard means and what it will look like if their students have mastered it. Often this conversation helps each of the team members come to a clearer understanding of what the standard means and whether it belongs on the power standards list.

For example, when an eighth-grade team discussed the new Common Core English Language Arts standards, one teacher suggested that the team look at how the literature and informational text standards were parallel. She suggested that teaching a certain concept (such as theme) would be easier in literature. Teachers could then build on the concept of theme when they taught it with informational text. Their consensus decision was to include it on their literature list but not on their informational text list. They believed their final product was much better than if they had just used a voting process.

It is very important that teams don't default to putting all of the standards that any single teacher thinks are power standards on the list as an easy way to satisfy everyone on the team. This compromise (rather than consensus) strategy will result in a final product, but it will likely have many more identified standards than the group wants, and the list won't be as effective as one built through the more difficult process of consensus. This consensus-building step may take some teams longer than others depending on how familiar team members are with their standards.

Some state standards are ambiguous and open to interpretation. By building consensus about power standards, teachers develop a common understanding of exactly what that standards mean. Consider, for example, this eighth-grade math standard: "Find the probability of compound independent events" (Cox, 2006, p. 18). Individual teachers might define *compound independent events* differently. In fact, they may have to look at released test items on the state website to understand exactly what this term means. Once they see that the problems the state uses involve flipping coins and rolling dice, they will have a better understanding of and make a better decision about whether it belongs on the power-standards list.

When the team has gone through each standard and decided whether to include it on the list, members have created their first draft. It is important that teachers understand that this is just a draft, and they have to complete the process to assure they have chosen the correct power standards.

The following example from a third-grade team shows this process of identifying power standards.

A team of four third-grade teachers at Longfellow Elementary met to begin the process of developing a draft of power standards for their grade. The team looked at the Common Core State Standards in the area of informational text (Common Core State Standards Initiative, 2010b, p. 14). During step one of the process, each teacher worked individually to identify which of the standards met one or more of the criteria (endurance, leverage, readiness) for a power standard. Teachers looked for approximately one-third of the standards to meet one of these criteria. One teacher on the team created the following list:

Key Ideas and Details

1. Ask and answer questions to demonstrate understanding of a text, referring explicitly to the text as the basis for the answers.

2. Determine the main idea of a text; recount the key details and explain how they support the main idea. (Endurance)

3. Describe the relationship between a series of historical events, scientific ideas or concepts, or steps in technical procedures in a text, using language that pertains to time, sequence, and cause/effect.

Craft and Structure

4. Determine the meaning of general academic and domain-specific words and phrases in a text relevant to a *grade 3 topic or subject area.*

5. Use text features and search tools (e.g., key words, sidebars, hyperlinks) to locate information relevant to a given topic efficiently. (Readiness)

6. Distinguish their own point of view from that of the author of a text.

Integration of Knowledge and Ideas

7. Use information gained from illustrations (e.g., maps, photographs) and the words in a text to demonstrate understanding of the text (e.g., where, when, why, and how key events occur). (Leverage)

8. Describe the logical connection between particular sentences and paragraphs in a text (e.g., comparison, cause/effect, first/second/third in a sequence). (Leverage)

9. Compare and contrast the most important points and key details presented in two texts on the same topic.

Range of Reading and Level of Text Complexity

10. By the end of the year, read and comprehend informational texts, including history/social studies, science, and technical texts, at the high end of the grades 2–3 text complexity band independently and proficiently.

The four members on the team saw that they each had items two and five on their individual lists of power standards, so they immediately included them on the team draft. Two teachers included item six on their lists, but after discussion, members agreed not to include it on the team list because they believed it would have been taught and mastered in second grade. They made a note to make sure it appears on the second-grade list when they meet to vertically align with other teams (vertical alignment is discussed in greater detail in the following section). One of the teachers had item ten on her list, so the team members debated whether to include it or not. They finally decided not to because they felt it was not something they would assess in isolation. (In fact, they decided to suggest that all of the teams need to have a discussion about the concept of text complexity and to make it a schoolwide focus.) After much discussion, the team decided to include items eight and nine on the team draft. Thus, the team's power standards draft was as follows:

1. Determine the main idea of a text; recount the key details and explain how they support the main idea. (Endurance)

2. Use text features and search tools (e.g., key words, sidebars, hyperlinks) to locate information relevant to a given topic efficiently. (Readiness)

3. Describe the logical connection between particular sentences and paragraphs in a text (e.g., comparison, cause/effect, first/second/third in a sequence). (Leverage)

4. Compare and contrast the most important points and key details presented in two texts on the same topic.

Aligning the Power Standards

Ainsworth (2004) recommends that the draft of standards then be aligned to what the state believes is important, as well as to the lists of power standards developed by the grade levels or courses taught before and after yours. States demonstrate what they think is important with emphasis, or lack of emphasis, on certain standards in their state tests.

One of the issues many teachers are concerned about when they go through this process is how their students will do on the high-stakes state test at the end of the year. As Ainsworth (2004) notes, Doug Reeves suggests:

> What you will find is that a good set of Power Standards will cover about 88 percent of the items on the state test, but not 100 percent. If you go after the extra 12 percent, you will have to cover many more standards and hence have less teaching time to thoroughly teach each of the Power Standards. (p. 97)

Reeves's recommendation is that students will do better on the state test as a result of more deeply understanding the most important standards.

One way that teachers can make sure their students have mastered the important content they will need to know for the state test is to make sure the power standards they've identified are aligned to what will likely be asked on the state test. Most states publish a "test blueprint" that lays out what percentage of questions on the state test will come from each standard area or strand area. If teams have an approximately similar percentage of power standards for these areas, they will be placing a similar emphasis on the standards deemed most important for the test.

If your team is unsure about what a standard means or what it will look like if your students know it, examine the curriculum frameworks and released test items from your state documents. You will also learn how difficult the questions are and what methods the test authors use to assess the standard.

Teams can also look at the results of their longitudinal data from their state, or other external tests, to see their typical weak areas. When one concept area has been weaker than other areas for a period of time, it may be because teachers aren't spending enough time on that concept or that their students don't have solid prerequisite skills. For example, if team members see that their students have been weak in the area of understanding informational text, then they should consider having a larger proportion of their power standards in that strand. Remember that having more power standards on a particular strand or concept means that the team will write common formative assessments and provide additional time and support to students for those standards. Thus, if students are less prepared coming in to the subject or grade level, they will get the support they need.

Another important step is for your team to check your list of power standards for vertical alignment. In this step, each of the teams in your school will share its list of power standards with the grade level before and the grade level after, or, in high schools, the course before and the course after. We have effectively accomplished this step by having each grade level bring its draft of power standards to a staff meeting on chart paper. Each team hangs its list in order by grade level. The staff then "walks the wall" looking for gaps and redundancies. The easiest to spot are the redundancies. This occurs when two or more teams have the same standard listed as a power standard. However, it's just as important for teams to make sure they don't have gaps where important standards have been left off all of the lists (Ainsworth, 2004).

Two or more grade levels may have a similar standard, but the level of rigor or complexity of thinking may be different. This is evident when the verbs used to describe the expected student performance move up the level of Bloom's Taxonomy. For example, one grade may be expected to *identify* figurative language in a passage, and the next grade may be asked to *analyze* the meaning of a sentence using a figurative-language phrase. To assure that they are not teaching the same standards, teams must look carefully at the expectations from grade level to grade level or course to course to make sure they are increasing the expectations.

Where Do the Common Core State Standards Fit In?

If your team has already established power standards from your state standards, you may be wondering how the new Common Core State Standards can or should be used in your work on common formative assessment. If your state has approved the new standards, you will likely benefit from developing a "crosswalk" from the beginning, between your own power standards and the most important Common Core State Standards. This involves examining your current list of power standards to see how they match the Common Core State Standards. When you find a match, it will be important to check the verb indicating the level of rigor expected for students to demonstrate mastery. After matching the two lists, review the remaining Common Core State Standards using the criteria of endurance, leverage, and readiness for the next level of learning to see if there are new power standards to be added to your list. As this book is being published, many schools and districts working with the Common Core are finding that, while the standards may not be *accelerated*, they often have a higher level of cognitive demand than in previous state standards. Teams may find that they will need to change the expectations for students on their common formative assessments as a result. We believe that this process will help teams in their own learning about what the standards mean and what proficiency will look like.

Time Is an Important Factor

Once your team has created a list of power standards, it is important to decide when to teach each of them and how long it will take. This step requires you to make sure you can fit all of what you believe is important into the time you have to teach it.

Pacing guides do not have to be written so tightly that teachers have to be teaching the same lesson on the same day, but it is important that one teacher doesn't take considerably longer to teach the same content because then he or she won't be teaching it at the same depth.

Many schools and districts develop quarterly pacing guides that list the power standards to be taught and assessed during each quarter. As teams plan their units and develop their own common formative assessments, this pacing guide helps them to see which units must be covered each quarter. We are often asked about how common the pacing must be to make common formative assessments work. Starting with the end in mind, teams should decide when they want to administer common formative assessments. While the rigorous expectations for security that surround state tests don't apply to teacher-created, teacher-owned common formative assessments, we advise that these assessments be administered as close as possible in time for all students—the same day if possible. This way, teams can plan and execute their corrective instruction together. Then teachers can pace their instruction in their own classrooms so they are ready to give the common formative assessment on the agreed-on day.

Schoolwide or Districtwide Power Standards?

The decision of whether to identify power standards at each school or across the district is a decision that needs to be based on a variety of factors. The advantage of having each school do this work is that all teachers will have ownership in the final product. We also believe that the process itself helps build a shared understanding of what each of the standards means. On the other hand, if the power standards are decided by a representative group of teachers from across the district, they will help assure a more common district curriculum. They can be used to write district benchmark assessments because all teachers who teach a particular grade level or subject will be teaching that standard at the same time. If the district does this work with a representative group, it is important that all teachers have an opportunity to review and provide feedback on the list of power standards before the final decision is made. Larry Ainsworth (2004) describes an "accordion process" that districts can use to gather input regarding power standards. In the first part of the accordion process, the representative teacher team drafts power standards. The accordion then expands out as the draft documents are sent to the schools for review and feedback. The accordion then comes back in, and the original team reviews and integrates the feedback. Finally, the accordion expands once more to send out the final drafts.

The Sample Agenda for Determining Power Standards (page 102 in the Tools for Teams appendix) shows a sample of the process a team might go through to determine its power standards, including the time frame for each step. Note that the process will likely *not* all happen during the same meeting.

Use, Review, and Rewrite

The process of deciding what is most important to teach is not finished after teams go through this entire process because they must use the power standards and be reflective about them for a period of time to assure they've chosen the correct standards. As teams work together throughout the first year with their initial list of power standards, they will discover that they have forgotten some important standards and some they've included should be cut. Your team should keep track of these new understandings so that you can revise your list for the following year.

You'll also discover that after a few years, as students move through grade levels with this common set of essential outcomes, they will be more consistently prepared for your course or grade level. Teachers will find they are spending less time in review and on prerequisite skills and more time teaching the most important concepts.

Remember that your list of power standards is the foundation for the rest of the work your team will do around common formative assessments. You may take longer than you expect to reach consensus on your first draft of power standards. This is important work and worth the time it takes.

CHAPTER 4

The Unwrapping Process— Achieving Collective Clarity on Learning Targets

KEY POINTS

- Standards are often written in terms that might be interpreted differently from teacher to teacher.
- The unwrapping process is a strategy to achieve collective clarity and agreement regarding specific learning targets contained within the standards.
- By identifying specific learning targets through the unwrapping process, teams will be prepared to design aligned and accurate assessment items.

Chapter 3 described a process that teams can use to filter the vast number of standards to determine which are most essential—the *power standards*. By determining the power standards, teams can obtain a collective focus on what it is that all students must learn, and, subsequently, what learning they will monitor with common formative assessments. However, just distinguishing the standards that are essential to know from those that are nice to know doesn't mean that everyone on your team will have the same interpretation of those standards, nor will it be easy to align your assessments with the standards as written.

Ever since schools began working with standards, whether national, state, or local, educators have struggled to make sense of their intent. Quite often, teachers tackle this work on their own, and their independent examinations result in interpretations that differ significantly from their colleagues in the classrooms next door—even if they teach the same grade level or course. As a result, their students receive instruction focused on different aspects of the standard, and the expectations relative to how students demonstrate proficiency differ as well. Why does this happen? First, the standards are typically written as a conglomeration of skills and knowledge that provide a broad—and sometimes very ambiguous—picture of proficiency to be achieved by the end of the school year. Second, the standards often use terms that are difficult to measure, such as *understand* or *know*, so it would be easy for teachers to interpret them very differently. Third, teachers use their individual background information and knowledge of the content area, which of course differs from one individual to the next.

The effective schools research highlights the notion that teachers within highly effective schools are clear on what students should be learning and consistently deliver the intended curriculum. In fact, researcher Robert Marzano (2003) ranks "a guaranteed and viable curriculum" as the number-one factor that raises student learning. Likewise, Wiggins and McTighe (2005) emphasize the importance of teachers being clear about the learning goals they will target within their instruction and assessment.

To truly answer the question, How do we know they are learning?, teams need a tool to achieve clarity concerning the question, What do we want students to know? The unwrapping process is just that tool. Unwrapping reveals the learning targets contained within the standards. By unwrapping the standards as a team, each member walks back to his or her classroom with the same picture of what students should know and be able to do, and, consequently, the same expectations for student learning. James Popham (2003) puts it best when he states:

> Teachers who truly understand what they want their students to accomplish will almost surely be more instructionally successful than teachers whose understanding of hoped-for student accomplishments are murky. (p. 16)

When a team moves forward in its accurate assessment of learning targets and takes action to ensure that students are actually attaining the skills and concepts, it has exemplified a true guaranteed and viable curriculum.

Throughout your teaching, you may have heard or experienced a similar process to what we're describing in this chapter. Wiggins and McTighe (2005) describe *unpacking* and Stiggins et al. (2004) describe *deconstructing*. They all mean basically the same thing and have the same goal in mind: getting a clear picture across all members of the team on the things we want our students to know and be able to do—in other words, the learning targets contained within the standard.

As you will see within this chapter, in addition to this common instructional clarity, the unwrapping process also sets the stage for creating *aligned* and *effective* common formative assessments. And in the end, after implementing your common formative assessments, your team will be able to make a true "apples to apples" comparison upon looking at the results. Let's take a look at how your team can get to this place.

Looking at the Structure of Your Standards

Currently, there is great variation from state to state and even from content area to content area in how standards are structured. Typically, there is some type of framework expressed in terms of *strands* or *domains*. The framework can be viewed as the closet organizer for the content of the standards: organized within each strand or domain are the content standards. In most states, these are accompanied by *performance indicators*—the grade-specific learning outcomes that support the attainment of each standard.

In most schools, grade-level or course teams have examined their standards and are familiar with their structure; however, if your team hasn't had the opportunity to do so, we strongly recommend examining how your standards are structured. Become familiar with the nuances and any additional documents or explanations that might be available to help clarify the expectations for students. For example, some states have written extensive curriculum frameworks that provide additional insight regarding the intent of the standard or developed exemplars that communicate the expected quality of student work. If you work in an elementary setting, for example, and are required to teach multiple content areas, you may find that some standards are written in terms that are broad and overarching while others are written with a high level of specificity. Taking advantage of these resources will help to create a clear picture in the team's mind about what students are expected to know and be able to do.

As we mentioned in chapter 3, states also structure their standards differently, although at the time of this writing, many are in the process of adopting Common Core State Standards. For example, the state of Massachusetts has categorized its history and social science standards based on their application to the major domains of history, geography, economics, and civics and government. Within each standard, each domain is referenced through a coding system: (H) history, (G) geography, (E) economics, and (C) civics and government.

Here is a third-grade standard from the Massachusetts standards:

> 3.3 Identify who the Pilgrims were and explain why they left Europe to seek religious freedom; describe their journey and their early years in the Plymouth Colony. (H, G, C, E)
>
> A. the purpose of the Mayflower Compact and its principles of self-government
>
> B. challenges in settling in America
>
> C. events leading to the first Thanksgiving
>
> (Massachusetts Department of Education, 2003, p. 20)

In contrast, the state of Texas has organized its social studies content standards by eight strands: history; geography; economics; government; citizenship; culture; science, technology, and society; and social studies skills. Its standards reflect both a global standard and specific indicators.

The following is an example from sixth-grade geography from the Texas standards:

> The student uses maps, globes, graphs, charts, models, and databases to answer geographic questions. The student is expected to:
>
> (A) create thematic maps, graphs, charts, models, and databases depicting various aspects of world regions and countries such as population, disease, and economic activities;
>
> (B) pose and answer questions about geographic distributions and patterns for selected world regions and countries shown on maps, graphs, charts, models, and databases; and
>
> (C) compare selected world regions and countries using data from maps, graphs, charts, databases, and models.
>
> (Texas Education Agency, 2010, p. 2)

Regardless of the state in which you teach, all standards contain two distinct elements:

1. A set of concepts that students must ultimately know or understand

2. A set of skills that students should be able to perform

Within cognitive psychology, these two elements are referred to as declarative knowledge and procedural knowledge. *Declarative knowledge* describes what students should know. The declarative knowledge targeted within a standard may be related to concepts and ideas, such as the concept of democracy, or it can focus on specific content, such as the sequence of events leading up to World War II. *Procedural knowledge* refers to what students should be able to do with their knowledge, such as comparing the governmental structures of two countries.

In addition to describing the knowledge and skills students must attain, many standards also communicate the context or conditions in which students would know these concepts and be able to perform the skills. Consider the following standard from the first-grade mathematics Common Core State Standards (Common Core State Standards Initiative, 2010c, p. 15):

> Solve word problems that call for addition of three whole numbers whose sum is less than or equal to 20, e.g., by using objects, drawings, and equations with a symbol for the unknown number to represent the problem.

This standard makes it very clear that students will be given problems that might use objects, drawing, or equations to demonstrate their learning. This contextual information brings clarity to both instruction and assessment.

Regardless of how your standards are structured, here's the bottom line: your team needs to have a process to establish a common picture of the concepts, skills, and context in which your students are expected to be proficient. Unwrapping the standards is that process.

Unwrapping the Standards

Before we describe the process, let's clarify which standards your team should unwrap. First, we want to clarify that we are *not* recommending that you unwrap every standard in your grade level or content area. To do this would take at least a full year, and it is not the best use of your team's time. When identifying standards for formative assessment, your focus should be on those standards that are most essential for your team to monitor. As a team, you've already gone through a process of identifying your power standards, which has distinguished the *must knows* from the *nice to knows*. Your focus for formative assessments should be on those power standards. As a team, you will consider your upcoming segment of instruction, whether it be a unit or chapter, and decide which power standards you will address and monitor during that time period. Here's the unwrapping process, step by step.

Step One: Focus on the Key Words

After deciding which standard to focus on, the first step teams can take to achieve collective clarity on the standard is to break it down and organize the information. As a first step in unwrapping, Larry Ainsworth (2003) recommends doing the following with your standard:

1. Circle the words that depict the skills; in other words, circle the things students should be able to do (which are expressed as verbs) that are contained within the standard.

2. Underline the words that indicate the knowledge or concepts that students should know (expressed as nouns) that are the focus of the standard.

Finally, we also recommend putting brackets around any context information that may be provided within the standard.

Your team may use any variation of this process, but the key is to look closely at the standard and illuminate its essence—what it's really trying to say. This may sound a little awkward or contrived at first, but by highlighting key words contained within the standard, you will ensure that everyone on the team is focused on the same skills and concepts.

Here's an example from the Common Core State Standards for fifth-grade English language arts (2010b, p. 14):

> Compare and contrast the overall structure (e.g., chronology, comparison, cause/effect, problem/solution) of events, ideas, concepts, or information in two or more texts.

Now here's the standard with the key words highlighted (we've circled the skills and underlined the knowledge or concepts to be taught and assessed during instruction). We've also put brackets around the information that describes the context, or conditions, in which those skills and concepts are demonstrated.

(Compare) and (contrast) the <u>overall structure (e.g., chronology, comparison, cause/effect, problem/solution) of</u> [events, ideas, concepts, or information in two or more texts].

Step Two: Map It Out

Once you've identified the key skills and concepts contained within the standard, and any context in which they will be attained, work as a team to organize them in a way that makes sense. There are many variations of graphic organizers that you'll see in this chapter, but let's begin with table 4.1 in which the standard has been broken down to reveal two major skills: compare and contrast, which require specific concepts and knowledge.

Table 4.1: Option One With Two Major Skills

What Will Students Do? (Skills)	With What Knowledge or Concepts?	In What Context?
Compare	overall structure (chronology, comparisons, cause/effect, or problem/solution)	of two or more texts that contain events, ideas, concepts, or information
Contrast	overall structure (chronology, comparisons, cause/effect, or problem/solution)	of two or more texts that contain events, ideas, concepts, or information

Tables 4.2 and 4.3 (page 42) show alternate ways teams might graphically organize the same type of information. Note that the key areas of skills, concepts, and context information are still addressed, regardless of the different layout.

Table 4.2: Option Two With Two Major Skills

What Concepts Do Students Need To Know?	What Will They Be Able to Do With These Concepts?	In What Context?
Textual structure of chronologies Textual structure of cause/effect Textual structure of comparisons Textual structure of problem/solution	Compare (chronologies, comparisons, cause/effect, problem/solution texts)	of two or more texts that contain events, ideas, concepts, or information
	Contrast (chronologies, comparisons, cause/effect, problem/solution texts)	of two or more texts that contain events, ideas, concepts, or information

Table 4.3: Option Three With Two Major Skills

		In What Context?
Concepts students need to know	Textual structure of chronologies Textual structure of cause/effect Textual structure of comparisons Textual structure of problem/solution	of two or more texts that contain events, ideas, concepts, or information
Skills they need to be able to do	Contrast (chronologies, comparisons, cause/effect, problem/solution texts) Compare (chronologies, comparisons, cause/effect, problem/solution texts)	of two or more texts that contain events, ideas, concepts, or information

It is not absolutely necessary that each member of the team use the same graphic organizer. Some may prefer using one of these templates, while others may actually create their own system that organizes the skills and concepts. Keep in mind what Larry Ainsworth (2003) says:

> There is no one right way to "unwrap" standards in terms of organization and format. The only important criterion is for colleagues to remember when "unwrapping" the same standards and indicators is to make sure that the same key concepts and skills appear on each educator's graphic organizer. (p. 21)

By organizing the information stated in the standard, it's clear that students will be taught two different skills, comparing (finding things that are the same) and contrasting (finding things that are different). Conceptually, they will need to identify the type of overall structure depicted within the structure of two or more texts.

Additionally, we recommend that teams highlight the academic language that will be taught and monitored during the instruction. This reinforces that your students, especially those learning a new language or struggling with vocabulary, are provided explicit instruction in academic language, and that their attainment of those concepts is monitored. In the example in the tables, academic language includes the terms *chronology*, *cause/effect*, *problem/solution*, *compare*, and *contrast*.

When Things Get "Muddy": Dealing With Vague or Ambiguous Learning Targets

Some standards are written in a way that makes it absolutely clear to the reader the skills and concepts students should be able to do within a certain context. However, quite often, standards are expressed in extremely broad or vague terms, or in a way that is difficult to measure. Following are some considerations for teams working with standards that fall into either of these categories.

Identify implied learning targets—One of the benefits of unwrapping standards as a team is that you will not only get clarification on what is written in the standards but also on what is *not* written. Most of us have seen "umbrella standards"—standards written in such broad terms that they encompass a large number of skills and concepts. Standards written in this way rely greatly on teachers' ability to identify the subset of learning targets based on their content knowledge and prior experience. As a result, the implied skills and concepts leading to the standard might be perceived and addressed quite differently from teacher to teacher. To ensure that students are guided through the instructional process without significant gaps in concepts and skills, teachers must work together to fill in the gaps in the standards. Consider the following fifth-grade standard:

Describe how various non-economic factors (e.g., culture, values, interests) can influence economic behaviors and decision making. (North Dakota Department of Public Instruction, 2007, p. 6)

To effectively break down this very broad standard into teachable and measurable increments, teams should discuss and clarify the sequence—in other words, identify the learning targets that are implied, but not explicitly mentioned. In some ways, the process reflects a *task analysis* of the big standard: it breaks the large target down into smaller learning targets that fill the gap between initial instruction and the end result described by the broad standard.

For the fifth-grade example, those implied learning targets might be:

- Distinguish between culture, values, and interests.

- Identify isolated factors at work within a situation (such as culture, values, and interests).

- Identify multiple factors at work within a situation.

- Summarize the influence of factors on decisions made within a scenario.

Clarify unmeasurable targets with verb substitution—Occasionally, your team may encounter standards that contain unmeasurable terms, such as *understand* or *know*. While we wholeheartedly endorse the use of technology in the classroom, we know of no high-tech tool that automatically measures a student's knowledge or understanding! We need to convert such standards into clear learning targets that are tangible *and* measurable. Remember, the goal is clarity! One strategy for clarifying these vague learning targets is to substitute verbs such as *know* or *understand* with replacements that are observable and measurable. For example, consider the following fifth-grade standard:

Understand how the British colonial period created the basis for the development of political self-government and a free-market economic system, and the differences between the British, Spanish, and French colonial systems. (California State Board of Education, 1998, p. 18)

Here's the unwrapped standard with substitutions:

- ~~Understand~~ *Paraphrase* the basis for:
  - Influence of colonial period on political self-government
  - Free-market economy
- ~~Understand~~ *Contrast* the differences among colonial systems:
  - British colonial system
  - Spanish colonial system
  - French colonial system

Replacing the word *understand* will not only help your team gain clarity in what to target as a skill but it will also jump-start the conversation about potential strategies for assessment. For example, in the sample standard, the substitution of *paraphrase* and *contrast* could lead the team to the idea of using a written assessment to describe the development of political self-government in the British colonial period, or a visual map, such as a Venn diagram, to compare and contrast the colonial systems.

Step Three: Analyze the Target

Now that you've broken down and organized the standard, take a look at the skills that emerged to determine the level of thinking the standard targets. We recommend that teams use a common framework to examine the level of thinking in order to build consensus. Doing so will empower the team to begin distinguishing between simple and complex learning targets, which, as you'll discover later on, will serve you well as you create a scoring rubric.

Following are the three most common frameworks used to examine the level of thinking within learning targets:

1. Bloom's Taxonomy for Learning (Revised; Anderson & Krathwohl, 2001)

2. Marzano's Taxonomy (Marzano, 2000)

3. Webb's Depth of Knowledge (DOK; Webb, 2005)

We recommend that you use whichever framework is most familiar to you and your colleagues. Table 4.4 shows a comparison of the same learning target (from the Common Core State Standards for grade 4, numbers and operations in base ten) across all three frameworks.

Table 4.4: Sample Analysis of a Learning Target's Level of Thinking Using Three Frameworks

Learning Target	Bloom's Taxonomy (Revised) Describes cognitive processes based on their intellectual demand	Marzano's Taxonomy Describes six levels of mental processing	Webb's Depth of Knowledge Describes the degree of understanding a student needs to respond to an assessment item
Compare two multidigit numbers based on meanings of the digits in each place, using >, =, and < symbols to record the results of comparisons. (Common Core State Standards Initiative, 2010, p. 31)	Remembering Understanding **Applying** Analyzing Evaluating Creating	Level 1: Retrieval Level 2: Comprehension Level 3: Analysis **Level 4: Knowledge utilization** Level 5: Metacognition Level 6: Self-system thinking	Recall and reproduction (DOK 1) **Skills and concepts (DOK 2)** Strategic thinking/complex reasoning (DOK 3) Extended thinking/reasoning (DOK 4)

Why is it important for teams to examine and come to consensus about the level of thinking targeted within a standard? First, we want to make sure that the instruction guides students to *at least* that same level of thinking. If we gear our instruction below the intended level of thinking, we're really not teaching to the standard. Second, when we design our assessments, we want to ensure alignment of our assessment to instruction. For example, consider the following fourth-grade language arts standard (Common Core State Standards Initiative, 2010b, p. 12):

> Determine a theme of a story, drama, or poem from details in the text.

The level of thinking examined in this standard falls into the category of *analyzing* on Bloom's Taxonomy. However, if our assessment items are actually geared more toward *remembering* or *understanding*, the desired learning target and what's actually being assessed would not be aligned. Teams should set a goal of ensuring that there is a dot-to-dot connection between the learning targets, the instruction that takes place, and the assessment items that teams develop and implement.

While the completion of steps one to three in the unwrapping process will give teams what they initially need to begin creating common formative assessments, we recommend going further in your conversation about the learning targets by identifying the big ideas and essential questions related to your standards.

Step Four: Determine the Big Ideas

Grant Wiggins and Jay McTighe (2005), in *Understanding by Design*, describe big ideas as "linchpins," the pieces of equipment that hold the wheel on the axle. Big ideas hold conceptual knowledge and skills together and help the learner see and make connections. They represent the things you want students to really remember after you're done teaching specific concepts and skills—the *important to know* information. We like to think of them as the "forest versus the trees" or the "moral of the story."

Here are some examples of big ideas:

- Estimation helps us determine the reasonableness of an answer.
- The use of resources by humans impacts the ecosystems found in nature.
- Good communicators choose their words carefully.

As you can see, big ideas are brief, and since their goal is to ensure that students grasp the most essential and overarching concepts related to the content, they should be written in student-friendly, understandable language. This is where the team's professional expertise comes into play. You'll work as a group to identify the deep understandings that frame or encompass the learning targets. Here are some guiding questions to spark your team's ideas:

- What are the "V-8 ideas" (or "Aha" material) that we want every student to retain after our instruction?
- What concepts do we consider to be enduring understandings that extend beyond the instruction over time? In other words, do any of the concepts obtained in this unit have the potential for application in other areas of life?
- Do these big ideas serve as culminating nuggets of information?

Step Five: Establish Guiding Questions to Be Answered in Your Instruction

Guiding questions, sometimes referred to as *inquiry questions or essential questions*, help to focus and energize students during instruction. When structured effectively, guiding questions lead students to seek and acquire answers to the big ideas—they direct students' search for understanding. In fact, guiding questions are often answered by the big ideas (Ainsworth, 2003).

Here are some examples of guiding questions:

- How does the position of Earth in the solar system affect the conditions on our planet?
- What is healthy living?
- How can the structure of a text help us to understand information?

Putting It All Together

We have now gone through each of the five steps of unwrapping. The example in figure 4.1 puts all the steps together to show the process as a whole. It illustrates unwrapping of a fourth-grade Common Core standard targeting reading for information (Common Core State Standards Initiative, 2010b, p. 14):

> Explain events, procedures, ideas, or concepts in a historical, scientific, or technical text, including what happened and why, based on specific information in the text.

Step One: Focus on the Key Words			
(Explain) events, procedures, ideas, or concepts in a [historical, scientific, or technical text], including what happened and why, based on specific information in the text.			

Step Two: Map It Out			
What Will Students Do? (Skills)	**With What Knowledge or Concepts?**	**In What Context?**	**Step Three: Analyze the Target**
			Level of Thinking
Explain	what happened based on specific information in an event, procedure, or ideas/concept	contained in historic, scientific, or technical text	Remembering
Explain	why something happened based on specific information in an event, procedure, or idea/concept	contained in historic, scientific, or technical text	Understanding

Implied learning targets:

- Negotiate various text structures (such as historic, scientific, or technical text).
- Identify key ideas and information within a text.
- Summarize (orally or in writing).
- Recognize cause/effect relationships.

Vocabulary: Summarize, paraphrase

Step Four: Determine the Big Ideas
• There are strategies that good readers use to identify critical information in a text and communicate it effectively to others.

Step Five: Establish Guiding Questions to Be Answered in Your Instruction
• How does the way the information is arranged on a page assist me as a reader?
• What are strategies that help to organize information that I've learned so that I can share it with others?

*Visit **go.solution-tree.com/assessment** to download and print this figure.*

Figure 4.1: Example of the five-step process for unwrapping standards.

Getting Started as a Team

Now that you and your team have walked through the unwrapping process and seen some samples of unwrapped standards, it's time to give unwrapping a try. We recommend that teams begin by selecting one power standard on which they will focus during the upcoming instructional period. See the Sample Agenda for Unwrapping Standards on page 103 in the Tools for Teams appendix to help structure the work of your team as you begin unwrapping the standards. We provide two unwrapping templates in the Tools for Teams appendix. The first template, the Unwrapping Template (page 104), provides teams with a graphic organizer they can use to unwrap the standards. The second template, the Unwrapping Template for Backward Planning (page 105), will help your team apply this process to the planning of entire instructional units that may include multiple standards. Backward planning is discussed in detail in chapter 6.

We've Unwrapped Our Standards—Now What?

Hopefully, your team has found success using the unwrapping process to gain clarity about the skills and concepts the team will target in instruction and assessment. As you've probably figured out by now, the heart of the unwrapping process is in the conversations you've had as a team. There may have even been some challenging moments in which you struggled to reach agreement. This is to be expected. It's how we achieve an accurately and consistently delivered curriculum for our students.

You may have also noticed that the unwrapping process revealed multiple layers of skills and concepts your team will be teaching in the coming year. In chapter 6, we share how teams can benefit from mapping out those skills and concepts in a pacing guide. Additionally, you'll see how to use a unit-design approach to address skills and concepts in a more integrated fashion, again, helping to organize instruction across the year.

In the end, teams can ask themselves the following two guiding questions if they are wondering whether they've effectively completed the unwrapping process:

1. Do you feel that your team has clear direction on the concepts and skills that will be taught and assessed?

2. Did you get clarity on the academic language you want to reinforce in your instruction?

If the answer is yes, congratulations! You're ready to go into the next phase of your team's work and answer the question, How might we assess the learning targets we've identified through the unwrapping process? Chapter 5, Designing Quality Common Formative Assessments, will assist your team in answering this question.

CHAPTER 5

Designing Quality Common Formative Assessments

After reading and using the strategies in chapter 4, you and your team know how to achieve a better understanding of your state standards and, through the unwrapping process, how to uncover the learning targets that are most important for your students to learn. Uncovering these targets is the important first step to designing quality assessments because the targets to be assessed must be clear to both the student and the teachers. This chapter focuses on the next critical step in the process: designing assessments, including writing or choosing good items, knowing what to include in the assessment, and making sure the data you collect will really help your team know what to do next to help your students.

Have you ever felt that you don't have the knowledge to design quality assessments that will effectively tell you whether or not your students have learned the skills and concepts you've been teaching? Most teachers have felt this way, perhaps because they are aware of the level of statistical analysis large test-writing companies perform, and they wonder how their skills can compare. However, assessments designed by classroom teachers that are intended to reveal what students have learned and what they need to know next around specific learning targets don't have to use the same level of statistical analysis as high-stakes tests used to determine AYP, graduation, or college entrance. Thus, for classroom teachers, it's not necessary to use what Doug Reeves (2007) calls "psychometric perfection" (p. 235). In fact, he suggests that the benefit of getting information quickly and easily by using frequent formative assessments outweighs the risks of not writing perfect assessments. He believes that because these formative assessments are done so frequently, unintended errors will be caught quickly. That is, if a student is identified as needing more help and actually understands the target of learning, the student can quickly demonstrate learning during the corrective instruction time. Also, if a student looks like he is proficient on a target of learning, but actually isn't proficient, teachers will catch that error as they do more assessment. Of course, our goal is to make sure our assessments are as accurate as possible so that we gather good information from the beginning.

Most teams want to know how to develop practical, easy-to-use assessments that provide information about student learning and help determine next steps for classroom instruction—assessments that are valid and reliable, but that don't rely on difficult design strategies and statistical analysis.

Therefore, let's consider what the terms *valid* and *reliable* mean for common assessments. *Valid* implies that the assessment is truly measuring what the team thinks the students have learned. For example, if your team has been working toward students learning the science concept "permeability across a membrane," the assessment must tell your team which students know and understand that concept and which students haven't yet learned it. Equally as important, the assessment must measure student learning at the thinking level the team has set for student mastery. That is, your team may want students to know the definition of *permeability*, as well as to be able to describe what it means—what it looks like at a cellular level. The assessment must be designed to measure both of these thinking levels.

Teams also want to know that their assessments are *reliable*—that the students who appear to have learned the concept have actually learned it, and that the students who appear to not have mastered it truly haven't. They want to know that the results they are getting are accurate, so that they can make decisions about what to do next that will improve student learning.

Most importantly, your team wants to design quality assessments that *don't* require statistical analysis after they are administered to assure they are both valid and reliable. Rather, it wants to use a process that is set up from the beginning to assure accurate results.

There are some specific strategies your team can use for designing common formative assessments to assure you are getting the right information about what you have taught—information you can use to know what to do next for your students. This chapter presents a five-step process for designing quality assessments.

Step One: Decide What to Assess

In chapter 4, you learned how to unwrap state standards to get a better understanding of their meaning. As part of that process, you uncovered specific learning targets that your team discussed in depth, agreeing on which were most important to teach, as well as the expected thinking level for students for each target. The targets you identify as the most important become the basis for your common formative assessment plan. Formative assessments are written around these specific learning targets, rather than around state standards. However, your team does not have to assess each learning target it has identified—only those determined to be critical for students to know and be able to do. This means the team will view some of the unwrapped targets as either less important or as scaffolding skills that lead to the understanding of another target. The team decides which targets have the most value and designs the assessment around those targets.

Let's look at an example. At Emerson Elementary, the fifth-grade team is teaching the following Common Core State Standard in math:

Add and subtract fractions with unlike denominators (including mixed numbers) by replacing given fractions with equivalent fractions in such a way as to produce an equivalent sum or difference of fractions with like denominators. (Common Core State Standards Initiative, 2010c, p. 36)

Team members know there are likely to be questions on the state tests that ask students to add fractions with like and unlike denominators, and perhaps to add mixed numbers as well. Depending on how the state displays student data, teachers may be able to identify students who have difficulty with this standard, but they are unlikely to know *why* students didn't understand.

Consider, instead, what would happen if this team created a common formative assessment that would provide better information, leading to stronger interventions. Using the process of unwrapping explained in chapter 4, the team unwraps the standard and lists all of the learning targets a student needs to know to be able to add and subtract fractions, including knowing the terms *numerator* and *denominator*, understanding what fractions with like and unlike denominators are, knowing how to find the least common denominator, and understanding and being able to apply the algorithm to add fractions (convert all fractions to their equivalent fractions with a common denominator, add the numerators, and keep the same denominator). The team decides to give a short common formative assessment after teachers have taught students to find the least common denominator. Based on the results of this assessment, teachers will easily be able to group students together who didn't understand that specific learning target and provide them with more time and support. Had they waited until the end of the unit and given a test on adding and subtracting fractions, they would know which students didn't understand how to add and subtract fractions, but not why they didn't understand.

To determine what to assess, look at the learning targets your team identified for one unit of instruction through the unwrapping process. Consider which of these learning targets have the most impact on student learning. The following questions will help you decide:

- Which targets are most likely to cause certain students difficulty?
- Which targets are prerequisite skills for information to come later in this unit?
- Which targets are absolutely necessary for students to know?

Once you have identified the most important learning targets, your team must discuss the critical issue of cognitive demand—what level of thinking do we expect from our students for each learning target? Without this important conversation, your assessments might not meet the criteria for being valid.

The next step is for your team to design an assessment plan for that unit of instruction: decide how many formative assessments to give, when to give them, and which specific learning targets to include in each assessment.

Step Two: Decide How to Assess

When designing an assessment plan for a unit, your team should consider a variety of assessment strategies. Although assessment experts use different names for these strategies, they generally fit into three categories: selected response, constructed and extended written response, and performance assessments.

Selected response generally defines assessment items that ask students to select the correct answer from information provided to them. Examples include multiple-choice, matching, and true/false questions (Ainsworth, 2006; Popham, 2003; Stiggins et al., 2004).

Constructed-response (also called *extended written-response* or *supply-response*) items are those that ask students to provide their own answer to a question or prompt (Ainsworth, 2006; Popham, 2003). These include short- and long-essay responses. However, not all constructed-response questions have to include writing. For example, teachers who ask their students to complete a graphic organizer (such as a Venn diagram) are using a constructed-response assessment.

Most assessment experts also recognize performance assessments as a type of assessment strategy (Ainsworth, 2006; Stiggins et al., 2004). Marzano (2010) calls these "oral reports and demonstrations." *Performance assessments* ask students to demonstrate their understanding of a learning target by performing in front of the teacher, who evaluates them against a rubric.

Finally, some experts discuss a fourth type of assessment in which the teacher holds a student conference to ask questions and uncover what students know about a topic. Stiggins et al. (2004) call this "personal communication," and Marzano (2010) calls it "probing discussions." While personal communication and probing discussions may make excellent formative assessments, they generally don't work for teams of teachers who are gathering common data about their students because they don't use scripted questions and won't produce team data that can be used for subsequent planning.

Sometimes teachers are concerned that they are not using the right type of assessments—that using selected-response items, for example, is inferior to using other assessment measures. Stiggins et al. (2004) address this issue by saying that "none of these methods is inherently superior to any other, and all are viable if used well." However, these experts do note that some assessment strategies work better in some situations than in others.

When deciding which type of assessment strategies to use, your team must consider how well each type will measure student learning of a particular learning target, as well as factors such as how quickly you will be able to get the assessment results back. In addition, because your team will develop and use these assessments, you must consider how effectively you will be able to collaboratively score assessments that rely on rubrics that might be used unevenly by different members of your team. (Collaborative scoring is discussed more thoroughly in chapter 7.)

Selected-response assessments (multiple-choice, fill-in-the-blank, matching, and true/false items) work well for formative assessments because they are easy to grade, so teams get their results back quickly. They also allow teams to use multiple measures for each learning target—in other words, several questions for each target. Even if a student misunderstands one of the questions, the assessment will still determine whether or not the student learned the information. However, experts note that it is difficult or impossible to assess very high-level thinking using this type of question (Ainsworth, 2006; Popham, 2003; Stiggins et al., 2004).

Selected-response assessments are a good choice if a team wants to quickly assess a concept and be able to respond to the needs of the students the next day. Unless the concept being assessed is complicated or involves high-level thinking, the team can design, administer, and score the assessment in a day or two.

Constructed or extended written-response items require more time for teachers to score, and the results of scoring can be uneven if teachers apply the rubric differently. In addition, students' skill at writing can skew the results: students who have difficulty writing may appear not to have learned some targets that they have, in fact, learned. However, Stiggins et al. (2004) remind teachers that "extended written response works well for assessing chunks of knowledge that interrelate, rather than individual pieces of knowledge assessed separately" (p. 170). If teams want to understand student thinking around a target, constructed responses are the best way to get at that information. Additionally, these types of assessments help teachers see misconceptions students have about important concepts. Math teachers often want to see the work involved when students solve a problem so that they can identify exactly what students misunderstood. Constructed-response items provide this type of information.

Many teams find that the Common Core State Standards expect students to be able to analyze and evaluate information—two high levels of thinking. Thus, they are deciding to use constructed-response items for their common formative assessments to assure they are assessing the students at the thinking level they are teaching in their classes.

Teams can use student work samples as constructed-response assessments if they are designed around specific learning targets. For example, a second-grade team gives its students blank clock faces and asks them to draw in the hands for specified times. A middle school science team provides a graphic of plant and animal cells and asks students to identify specific cell parts, and then asks them to explain how they are alike and how they are different. A high school geography team provides a map of a town and asks students to describe the relative location between two specified addresses. Any of these activities could be considered practice by individual teachers, or they could be used by teams of teachers to assess what students have (or have not) already learned.

It is important to note that when a team uses student work samples for assessment purposes, those samples must be done individually by students. A group activity or group product does not provide sufficient information about individual students and thus cannot be used as an assessment.

Students often find performance assessments to be especially engaging. These assessments ask students to carry out a process while the assessor determines, usually using a rubric, the quality of the performance. Additionally, students may be asked to create a product that will also be evaluated against a rubric. This is often the most accurate way to assess students' ability to perform skills (Stiggins et al., 2004). However, performance assessments also take time to administer, and teams must plan ways to keep the rest of the class engaged while the teacher is watching and scoring each performance. Also, teams must develop the rubric together and discuss the nuances of its application to assure consistent evaluation.

Step Three: Develop the Assessment Plan

When developing an assessment plan, your team should consider each identified learning target, decide how to assess that particular target, and decide how long the whole assessment will take to administer.

Designing the Assessment

When developing an assessment plan, teams should consider two important factors in assessment design: making sure that the important learning targets you have identified are included in the assessment and making sure the items you write are assessing student learning at the cognitive level you identified in your unwrapping template. A quality assessment is one that includes items written around targets that the team feels are the most important and assesses at the level of thinking the team has agreed is important. Be aware, though, that in some cases, there might be more than one level of thinking to be included around a learning target. For example, a sixth-grade science team teaching a unit on the scientific method might want to make sure that students know what a hypothesis is, that they can make a hypothesis about a specific question or problem, and that they know the steps in the scientific method. Teachers will first assess student understanding of the term *hypothesis*. On the same assessment, they will assess whether students can apply this understanding to a specific situation. The team then decides what kinds of items to use to assess each of those areas. The assessment plan in this case will look like the example in table 5.1.

Table 5.1: Sample Assessment Plan for a Sixth-Grade Team

Learning Target	Knowledge	Application	Analysis	Evaluation
Understand hypothesis, and apply it to a given situation.	Four multiple choice	Two constructed response		
Know the steps of the scientific method.	Five matching questions			

In another example, table 5.2, a third-grade team wants to know whether its students can read an informational text passage about Asian and African elephants and see that the author has used the text structure "compare and contrast."

Table 5.2: Sample Assessment Plan for a Third-Grade Team

Learning Target	Knowledge	Application	Analysis	Evaluation
Identify and use the text structure of an informational text piece to aid comprehension.	Four multiple choice	One constructed response (Venn diagram)		

For the assessment, the teachers might ask their students to read a short essay about how these elephants are alike and how they are different. Then they might ask several multiple-choice questions about elephants that rely on the students being able to comprehend the passage. In addition, they might give their students a Venn diagram and ask students to complete it using the information in the text.

This short formative assessment allows teachers to see whether or not students can demonstrate that they comprehend the text by answering the multiple-choice questions correctly, but it also allows them to see that the students can pick out details from the text and put them in the compare or contrast portion of a Venn diagram.

While many teams will be comfortable developing their common formative assessments around only the learning targets being taught in their unit, your team may want to create assessment items that actually assess your students at a level beyond proficient so that you can measure your most able students and know which ones will benefit from additional enrichment activities during a particular unit. If this is the case, your team should consider designing the assessment with some items intended to assess a higher level of thinking beyond what you've identified as proficiency.

Robert Marzano (2010) describes one way to construct formative assessments so they include measuring learning targets at a level beyond proficiency. He suggests that teachers create an assessment rubric with a five-level scale: zero to four points. He describes the top level (four points) as "students make adaptations and inferences that go beyond what is explicitly taught at the score 3.0 level" (p. 51). To assess this level, teams must add items to their assessment that are designed to assess thinking at a level higher than they would expect all students to be able to learn.

Consider, for example, the fourth-grade team at Elm Place Elementary, where teachers have been teaching to the Common Core State Standard "Explain the meaning of simple metaphors and similes (e.g., 'pretty as a picture') in context" (Common Core State Standards Initiative, 2010b, p. 29). In addition to the items that ask students to identify similes and metaphors from a piece of text, and to explain what those similes and metaphors mean, the teachers also added a constructed-response question asking students to develop a narrative paragraph that includes the use of both a simile and a metaphor. This item will help teachers identify students who have exceeded the evidence of proficiency and who could benefit from some additional enrichment on figurative language. In this example, the Elm Place teachers will use the additional constructed-response question to sort out their students who can benefit from an extension activity while other students continue to work toward proficiency on the learning target. Their assessment plan would look like the example in table 5.3.

Table 5.3: Sample Assessment Plan for a Fourth-Grade Team

Learning Target	Knowledge	Application	Analysis	Evaluation
Identify similes and metaphors from text.	Five matching			
Explain the meaning of common similes and metaphors.		Four multiple choice		
Develop a narrative paragraph with both a simile and a metaphor.			One constructed response	

This team would then be able to use the results of the constructed-response item to identify which students are able to go beyond the anticipated learning targets identified by the team.

Considering the Sample Size: How Many Items Do I Need?

Stiggins et al. (2004) suggest that one important factor teachers must consider when designing assessments is the number of items to include. They must be sure to include enough so that they get accurate information about student mastery of learning targets. The more items used on an assessment, the more likely the results are to be reliable—that is, to provide accurate information about a student's knowledge around a learning target (Gareis & Grant, 2008). Gareis and Grant recommend three as the minimum number of questions or items for a learning target; they suggest that this gives a *triangulated* result; that is, the learning has been checked three times. This means that your results will be more accurate than if you relied on fewer questions.

Teams need to use a sufficient number of items to gather reliable information. They also must use formative assessments frequently. To accomplish both of these outcomes, it is important to keep assessments short. We recommend four selected-response items for each learning target if they are the only item type used. This way, a student could misunderstand or misread one of the questions and still achieve 75 percent accuracy if he or she knows the learning target. It is better practice, particularly for learning targets beyond basic-knowledge thinking, that teams use a combination of selected-response and constructed-response items.

Step Four: Determine the Timeline

Research has shown that the more frequently students are assessed, the more student achievement will increase (Bangert-Drowns, Kulik, & Kulik, 1991). However, your team must consider a variety of factors when deciding how often to administer common formative assessments. The first factor to consider is your timeline for responding with intervention/corrective instruction once you get back assessment results. For example, elementary teams with a common reading block during which students meet daily can regroup their students as often as once a week to respond to their needs as identified by assessments. In this situation, administering weekly assessments makes sense. However, if the team only has intervention/corrective instruction time for students once a week, it may make more sense for the team to administer common formative assessments every two to three weeks so that there is enough time to respond to students who need more time and support. In addition, the amount of common planning time a team has to write assessments, administer them, and analyze the data will also have an impact on assessment frequency. Keep in mind that teams that regularly do this work become more efficient than those just starting to learn the process.

We encourage teams to write and administer formative assessments at least every three weeks and as frequently as every week, with each formative assessment written around three learning targets or less. When teams use assessments with this frequency, the precision of the information they gather is much better, and therefore, their response with students is much better.

Step Five: Write the Assessment

There is a lot of information available about how to write quality assessment items. We offer some general guidelines to help you be certain your team is gathering reliable information about what students have learned.

Writing Selected-Response Items

A critical issue with selected-response items is that sometimes students who know the information answer incorrectly because they did not read or understand the question itself. When writing selected-response questions, teams should consider the following strategies to avoid confusing students:

- Include the entire question or statement in the stem of multiple-choice questions so students read through the entire statement before they begin to try to answer (Gareis & Grant, 2008; Popham, 2003; Stiggins et al., 2004). For example:

  Which of the following strategies will work best to assess students' ability to evaluate information from text?

  a.   Selected-response items

  b.   Constructed-response items

  c.   Performance items

- Use parallel construction for answer choices in multiple-choice questions (Gareis & Grant, 2008; Popham, 2003; Stiggins et al., 2004).

- Be cautious when choosing vocabulary or complex sentence structure (Stiggins et al., 2004). The following is an example of an item with sentence structure that confuses the test-taker:

Having difficult vocabulary in a question will often confuse students, which will reduce its reliability, so it's important to:

    a. Include a sufficient number of questions.

    b. Don't use vocabulary the students won't understand.

    c. Eliminate all questions that assess vocabulary.

- Use boldface type and italics for words that students might easily miss while reading the answer stem, such as *most likely* or *best choice* (Gareis & Grant, 2008; Stiggins et al., 2004).

- Write statements in the positive so the reader knows what the question is asking. For example, write, "Which one of the following is an example of . . ." rather than "Which one of the following is NOT an example of . . ." (Gareis & Grant, 2008; Popham, 2003).

- Keep the list short when writing matching questions. If you need to use more than one matching set, do so (Gareis & Grant, 2008; Popham, 2003; Stiggins et al., 2004). For example, you could break fifteen questions into two groups—one group with seven items and one group with eight items.

- Aim for the lowest possible reading level (Stiggins et al., 2004).

Because the purpose of the assessment is to determine what students still need help with, your team also must make sure students are unable to guess the correct answer in selected-response questions. Consider the following advice when writing these types of questions:

- Don't include "throw away" answer choices or choices intended to amuse students in multiple-choice questions. When students can easily eliminate an answer choice, their likelihood of being able to guess an answer is greater, thus making the data gathered less reliable (Gareis & Grant, 2008; Popham, 2003; Stiggins et al., 2004). While "eliminate the answers you're sure are wrong, and guess between the rest of the answers" is a skill students need to know for high-stakes testing, it is not something we want them to do on formative assessments.

- Make sure all answers for multiple-choice questions could possibly be correct, but that they are not so close to correct that a student who understands the content has a difficult time deciding the *best* answer (Gareis & Grant, 2008; Popham, 2003; Stiggins et al., 2004).

- Avoid equal-sized lists in matching questions so that students can't match all of the items they know and then guess between the leftover items (Gareis & Grant, 2008; Popham, 2003; Stiggins et al., 2004).

- Put answer choices in logical order (alphabetical, small to large) in selected-response questions so that students can't just guess where the answer might be. For example, you want to avoid students thinking, "There hasn't been a *b* response for a while, so I'd better choose *b* if I don't know the right answer" (Gareis & Grant, 2008; Popham, 2003; Stiggins et al., 2004).

When questions are multiple choice, some software programs generate an item-analysis report that teams can also use to help them plan follow-up for their assessment. The program will provide a list of which students chose each of the answers.

For example, when teams write a multiple-choice item, they might use the common misunderstandings students have about the learning target as the distracters (the wrong answer choices). By looking at the item analysis, teams know exactly why students missed that particular problem. Kopriva (2008) explores this approach by suggesting that there are three types of distracters teams might use when writing math problems. The first is a distracter that provides evidence the student didn't understand the question being asked, the second a distracter that is the result of a common misunderstanding about the problem being solved, and the third is the result of *backsolving*—trying out each possible solution. Your team may want to consider this approach to deciding what distracters to include.

Remember that the purpose of formative assessment is to determine what students know and what they are still experiencing difficulty understanding. By keeping these strategies in mind, your team can avoid getting bad data.

Writing Constructed-Response and Extended Written-Response Items

The recommendations for making selected-response questions easy to read and understand apply to constructed-response questions as well. However, the experts have some additional recommendations.

With constructed-response and extended written-response questions, it is important to give students a context to use for their answer (Gareis & Grant, 2008; Popham, 2003; Stiggins et al., 2004). For example, if students are asked to write about the effects of environmental issues on the future of the United States, remind them about specific issues, such as the 2010 Gulf of Mexico oil spill or the greenhouse effect created by car emissions. This helps them to frame how they will answer. The resulting question might be:

> Environmental issues can have social, economic, and political effects on our country. For example, the 2010 oil spill in the Gulf of Mexico affected our economy through the tourism industry—an economic effect. The greenhouse effect has resulted in many new laws reducing car emissions—a political effect. Choose one environmental issue that has had such an impact and explain what the social, political, and economic impact was.

In addition, make sure the question or prompt is novel—that is, make sure it isn't about a topic that you've already discussed in class (Gareis & Grant, 2008; Popham, 2003). For example, if you ask students to describe the effects of the Civil War on the economy of the South, and this was a topic of discussion during the unit, they are only being asked to remember what was discussed. However, if you ask them to describe how the economy of the North was affected (and this hadn't been discussed in class), the assessment determines whether students are able to understand the reasoning around this concept by applying it in the new circumstance.

Finally, make sure that the directions for the assessment are clear and easy to understand, and leave space for your students to fully answer the questions.

Designing Performance Assessments

Stiggins et al. (2004) recommend teams use performance assessments when the learning target is a skill that can best be assessed by observing the student perform that skill. He notes that with performance assessment, students should know how they will be evaluated (the scoring rubric) during their performance.

Students should not be given a choice between different performance tasks unless all tasks are the same level of difficulty and designed to assess the same learning targets. Otherwise, students could choose to do the task they know and understand and skip a task they don't know (Stiggins et al., 2004).

Additional Guidelines for Writing Assessment Questions

When writing assessments, teachers will often look for pieces of grade-level text they can use to assess reading comprehension. Remember that common formative assessments are generally written around specific reading skills or strategies. Therefore, the text must provide the appropriate opportunity to assess that strategy. For example, if the team has taught the text structure *cause and effect* and wants to see if students can analyze a piece of writing and use it to aid comprehension, then it must find a grade-level appropriate piece of text written in the cause-and-effect format. Textbook assessment materials and released materials from state tests (found on state websites) are places to look for text passages to include in assessments. In addition, appendix B in the English Language Arts Common Core State Standards provides a variety of suggested text pieces to use for assessing students on these standards.

Sometimes teams want to use questions from test banks, their textbooks, or other sources. When using these questions, teams must take some important steps to make sure these sources will yield accurate information about student learning. It is important that all questions are aligned to the learning target being assessed, and questions must also be written at the level of rigor set for that target. For example, if the learning target being assessed is that students can draw conclusions from data gathered in an experiment, it is important that the question isn't a simple knowledge question. Instead, students should be given a data set from an experiment and asked to write and explain what their conclusion is. In addition, it is very important for teams to consider the quality of the items they are selecting—just because they are provided by an outside source does not guarantee they will measure the learning targets identified by the team or that they are well written.

During the process of writing assessment questions, teams might wonder if they should use certain types of questions or structure them in a certain way to prepare students for high-stakes tests. Teams should discuss this issue to determine how to include these important strategies into their curriculum if they decide it's appropriate. Instead of using formative assessments for this purpose, many schools and districts use the benchmark assessments that measure student progress over a period of time to provide students with practice in test-taking strategies. These assessments are often written using items similar to those on the state test. Once the assessment has been given, the teachers can go back over the items to show students test-taking strategies they can use in the future.

One of the benefits of working collaboratively is that teams become better item writers and assessors by sharing ideas and information. Teams often want to know how to get started on this process and how to be as efficient as possible. Our first recommendation is that, at least early in your work, the entire team works together to plan and write the assessment. The value of learning together often outweighs the time it takes to create collaboratively. In fact, as teams get started they may take more time to design and write their assessments and find they can't complete as many assessments as they'd like. We believe that this initial learning process makes quality more important than quantity!

We do suggest, however, that teachers bring any assessments they've used in the past for consideration—you don't have to reinvent the wheel if it's already working. These assessments provide a starting point for the team's work. However, it is really important that the team completes the assessment plan first before choosing or writing items. Then, as the team writes the assessment, each teacher must make sure that students will understand and be able to read the included items. These multiple points of view will make it easier to spot confusing items.

We also strongly recommend that teams keep feedback from their already-administered assessments about what worked and what didn't. The following year, the team can then update the assessments rather than starting from scratch.

Step Six: Review the Assessment Before Administration

It is important for your team to review the assessment closely prior to giving it to students. Are the directions clear? Do students know what you are asking them to do and why? Some teams actually list the learning targets on the assessment itself, followed by the questions related to each target. This helps students to clearly understand the context of the questions. Teams should also review the expectations about how much time it will take to administer the assessment.

Step Seven: Set Proficiency Criteria and Decide How to Gather the Data

During this step, teams first discuss what proficiency will look like. For selected-response questions, decide how many correct responses students must have for each learning target. For example, if there are four multiple-choice questions, students who get at least three correct will be considered proficient. A scoring rubric is necessary to determine proficiency for constructed- and extended written-response items. For example, your team might decide that on a six-point rubric, a level four will be proficient.

There are two types of rubrics: holistic and analytic. A *holistic rubric* is used to score the overall proficiency of a student work sample or performance. An *analytic rubric* is used to evaluate each criteria or trait of the student work sample or performance separately to analyze student learning in a more specific way (Arter & Chappuis, 2006). The advantage of using an analytic rubric for a common formative assessment is that you will be able to determine exactly what areas of learning individual students need additional time and support in—as long as the rubric was designed around the specific learning targets. Chapter 7 discusses creating rubrics in greater detail.

In the next chapter, we'll discuss how teams can use their data to design units and pacing guides. Before teams can use their data for the bigger picture, though, they must gather and organize it. Because data analysis is done by learning target first, that is the structure by which the data must be gathered. Then your team will look at how each student did on each learning target. Teams can save time during their data team meeting by having a plan for how to gather data, as shown in table 5.4.

Table 5.4: Plan for How to Gather Data

Target	Students Who Need More Time and Support	Students Who Will Benefit From More Practice	Students Who Will Benefit From Enrichment or Extension
Target One			
Target Two			

Teams need to make sure their assessments are both valid (assess the expected learning targets at the anticipated level of thinking) and reliable (provide accurate information about what the students have learned). The Evaluating the Quality of an Assessment tool on page 106 of the Tools for Teams appendix will help you assess the quality of your assessments.

The Sample Protocol for Developing an Assessment tool in the Tools for Teams appendix on page 107 outlines the seven-step process for developing an assessment, highlighting the main tasks of each step. Your teams can use this tool for reference as you begin the process of developing your own common formative assessments. The team uses the Assessment Plan document on page 108 as it begins the process to decide which targets are being assessed and what the expected level of thinking is for those targets. It then completes the table by deciding what types of assessments to use and how many items it will need to include.

Final Thoughts

By thoughtfully designing assessments around specific learning targets and gathering and analyzing the data, your team will know exactly what your students have learned and what they are still experiencing difficulty understanding. This allows you to develop a strong instructional response to assure that the additional time and support you give to students will meet their learning needs. In chapter 6, we discuss creating pacing guides and designing units using the information you've gathered through the assessment process.

CHAPTER 6

The Big Picture—
Pacing Guides and Unit Design

KEY POINTS

- Pacing guides help teams plan for consistent and viable instruction of essential curriculum.
- The backward planning model is highly effective for designing instructional units that address multiple standards.
- Assessments are not isolated events—they are part of instruction, and they should be designed prior to instructional strategies.

So far, we have focused on how teams can identify and unwrap standards to reveal learning targets that they then monitor through the common formative assessments they create. This focus on single standards, however, is not typical in the real world of classroom instruction, where teachers don't usually teach one standard at a time. Rather, our instructional units tend to address a cluster of integrated standards. This chapter pulls back from the close-up view of single standards to examine the big picture. By examining strategies for establishing pacing guides and designing instructional units (what we like to call *learning plans*), we hope to support teams in the creation of long-range plans that not only embed common formative assessments but maximize their power on a larger scale. Consider the following scenario.

The eighth-grade science team at Forbes Middle School had recently identified its power standards. In addition, the school had recently identified a significant need in the area of critical reading and writing of informational text, and staff had made a commitment to intentionally support these skills within their content. The team rolled out a big sheet of butcher paper and quickly drew a template. Collaboratively, the teachers looked at the list of eighth-grade power standards and began organizing them around four-week instructional segments. Once they had plotted the science power standards, they went back and embedded literacy standards (such as writing and critical reading) that would be addressed within their instruction curriculum. In a relatively short time, they created a "big picture" pacing guide of their instruction for the first semester. This allowed them to focus their collective attention on design of the first instructional unit in which they would introduce students to concepts and skills related to experimentation and the scientific method. Together, they backward planned the four-week unit, which involved unwrapping the standards to reveal specific learning targets, and determined how and when they would embed common formative assessments that would tell them whether students attained the concepts and skills they were targeting. Each member of the team contributed to the design of the team's learning plan, which included specific strategies for instruction that had proven effective in the past. It also ensured that every student in the school had a solid foundation in the concepts and skills teachers would reference across the remaining instructional units in science that year.

From Isolated Standards to an Instructional Roadmap

One of the big ideas of a PLC is a focus on learning—ensuring high levels of learning for all students. To accomplish this goal, we examine the vast number of standards and prioritize them into what is essential learning for students. Then we determine how we will know when students have learned by designing assessments. Next, teams need a game plan—a way to teach all of the standards that is consistent and coherent, so that all students learn the concepts and skills that are most essential, regardless of which school they attend or which teacher they have. To set the stage for providing this coherent curriculum, we recommend that teams work together to create a blueprint, often called a pacing guide, of their year.

Pacing guides outline the sequence of instruction and describe when each standard (and the essential learning targets) will be addressed within a specified time frame. In our work with schools, we have seen great variety in the design and use of pacing guides. Some are extremely specific, noting exact pages from the textbook. Others are broad, describing when certain skills or concepts are to be addressed during the year, such as quarterly or by semester. According to Jane David (2008), the best pacing guides emphasize curriculum guidance instead of prescriptive pacing; they focus on central ideas and provide links to exemplary curriculum materials, lessons, and instructional strategies.

It should be noted that pacing guides do not need to be developed to address only one particular set of content standards. Many teams map the pacing of their instruction using an integrated approach. For example, a history/social studies team may also embed language arts standards, such as report writing, within its pacing guide. This integrated approach will likely support the implementation of the Common Core State Standards, which places significant emphasis on the integration of skills across content areas.

Finally, pacing guides are not meant to be written in stone or followed in lockstep fashion. We strongly encourage teams to use their professional expertise and examine results of their instruction in order to inform and refine the pacing of their instruction—in other words, they use evidence of student learning gathered through common formative assessments to make adjustments. If it's clear that students aren't grasping a particular concept that is considered essential, moving on serves only to broaden any knowledge gap and create a shaky foundation for future learning. To that end, we have seen some very effective pacing guides that build in time for corrective instruction and differentiation, providing a consistent structure for the first tier of their school's pyramid of interventions.

Developing a Pacing Guide

There is no one right way to create a pacing guide; however, all members of the team should be clear on the sequence of instruction of essential skills and concepts, as well as the time allotted for each. Not all learning targets should be given the same amount of instructional time. Teams must determine which skills and concepts are the most essential and structure instructional time accordingly.

The first step in designing a pacing guide is to map out the standards for the year, determining the approximate time frame needed to teach each cluster of concepts and skills using a graphic organizer or template. The standards can be organized into instructional segments or "chunks" which typically become the basis of instructional units.

Teams can begin the process of developing a pacing guide by examining the various resources available, such as the following:

- Standards framework
- Power standards
- Textbook pacing guides
- Professional expertise
- Existing curriculum maps and pacing guides
- School calendar and schedules of district benchmarks, statewide assessments, or other related activities

These sources of information will help you to begin mapping out the time frame for addressing the power standards within the instructional segments. Note that one of the resources listed is *professional expertise*. PLCs make decisions based on what works.

Teams in some content areas might choose to plan what instruction teachers will deliver on a weekly basis. For example, an algebra team may develop an explicit pacing guide that specifies when certain concepts and skills are introduced on a weekly basis. Other content areas, such as history/social studies, might plan their instruction across a few weeks. They have identified learning targets to be obtained by the end of that time, but may be addressing larger concepts that will develop over the course of those weeks.

To support these different approaches, we provide two completed graphic organizers that show how teams create pacing guides (figures 6.1 and 6.2). Figure 6.1 (page 66) shows instruction paced over several weeks. Figure 6.2 (page 67) shows instruction paced by week. While these are some typical ways to graphically organize the pacing of instructional content, your team can use any graphic organizer—a mind map, table, or even a simple list—for its creation. We provide a Pacing Guide Template in the Tools for Teams appendix (page 109) as an example of a graphic organizer that teams can use to create a pacing guide organized by day.

Certain concept and skill "families" evolve across time, and pacing guides should be designed to reveal those stair steps. Teams will use the unwrapping process to break them into smaller targets and organize them by increasing complexity that allows for scaffolding across the year. For example, at the beginning of the year students may be introduced to the concept of identifying an author's argument, and as time goes on, they will have a deeper understanding, examining and analyzing increasingly more difficult variations of the concept, and will be expected to apply their knowledge in different contexts with more difficult text.

Weeks	Content/Topics	Essential Standards to Address
One to four	Teach/review comprehension strategies. Teach narrative text organization. Use narrative text to supplement content area instruction (such as biographies, historical fiction, narrative nonfiction, legends, and fables).	Use appropriate strategies when reading for different purposes. Make and confirm predictions about text. Identify main events of plot, causes, and influences. Use knowledge of situation, setting, and character traits and motivation to determine causes of character action. Define and identify figurative language (simile, metaphor, hyperbole, and personification). Create multiple paragraph compositions with introductory paragraph, central idea and topic sentence, supporting paragraphs, and correct indention.
Five to eight	Continue focus on narrative text. Embed more writing and use of rubrics.	See weeks one to four, plus select a focus, organizational structure, and point of view based on purpose, audience, length, and format requirements.
Nine to twelve	Place emphasis on informational text. Use content textbooks, informational trade books, essays, editorials, newspaper or magazine articles, and online information in read aloud, in shared reading, and in guided reading. Teach text organization and application of comprehension strategies within informational text.	Identify structural patterns found in informational text. Use appropriate strategies when reading for different purposes. Make and confirm predictions about text. Evaluate new information and hypotheses. Compare and contrast information. Distinguish between cause and effect and fact and opinion. Follow multiple-step directions (technical).
Thirteen to sixteen	Continue emphasis on informational text. Use summary writing. Practice oral deliveries.	See previous weeks, plus locate information in reference texts by using organizational features (such as prefaces and appendixes).

Figure 6.1: Example of a first semester, fourth-grade literacy pacing guide organized in four-week segments.

Planning for Intervention

Some teams plan for intervention within their pacing guides and, ultimately, their unit plans. For example, if they plan to administer a common formative assessment after twelve days of teaching, they may plan for day thirteen to be an intervention/extension teaching day. They can then either exchange students across the team, or each teacher can keep his or her own students and respond to the data from the assessment.

9/9 to 9/17	9/20 to 10/7	10/8 to 10/29	11/8 to 11/19	11/29 to 12/10
Chapter 1	Chapter 2	Chapter 3	Chapter 4	Chapter 5
Foundations of algebra	Equations	Inequalities	Functions	Linear functions
Write the simplified form of repeated multiplication using powers. Simplify a numerical expression using the order of operations. Evaluate algebraic expressions (replace variables with given numbers, and use the order of operations to simplify the expressions).	Solve equations with one variable using multiplication and division. Demonstrate knowledge of multiplication and division properties of equality. Apply properties to determine ratios, and solve proportions. Solve two-step and multistep equations.	Graph inequalities (for example, $r > 3$). Read a graph to determine the inequality. Use addition, subtraction, multiplication, and division properties to solve two-step and multistep inequalities.	Find the domain and the range, and identify function. Write functions based on independent and dependent variables. Evaluate functions. Find the nth term of an arithmetic sequence.	Understand that a rate of change is a ratio that compares the amount of change in a dependent variable to the amount of change in an independent variable. Find slope by using the formula. Write an equation in a slope-intercept form.

Figure 6.2: Example of an algebra I pacing guide organized in weekly segments (representing one semester).

Other teams plan for regular intervention time during the school day. For example, in an elementary school, the team may have a reading intervention time every day or on several days of the week. The team uses this time to provide instruction and reteaching for all students based on their common formative assessments. In this case, the regular reading time continues, and students get their reteaching and enrichment during the intervention time slot. This time is fluid—that is, students move into and out of groups based on the results of their formative assessments.

Some middle schools and high schools have created an intervention period either daily or on multiple days during the week when students receive additional instruction around identified areas of need based on common formative assessments. Teams may have to prioritize how this time is used, as some students may need help in multiple subject areas. Again, the key is that the time is flexible and that students aren't placed into groups based on summative assessment, but rather common formative assessments that can be used to identify and correct any misconceptions or skills for students who have not attained at an acceptable level of mastery. In other schools, individual classroom teachers are responsible for providing intervention in a differentiated way as indicated by common formative assessments.

Either of these pacing guides allows individual teachers to apply their personal style to the initial instruction a student receives. While the team decides the pacing for each unit, and might even collaborate to determine powerful instructional strategies designed to get high levels of learning from students, individual teachers can still plan their own lessons. However, over time, because effective collaborative teams have used the collective inquiry process, including an examination of which instructional strategies are most effective, they will likely find themselves automatically incorporating many effective instructional strategies they've learned from other team members.

The collaborative creation of a pacing guide helps teams take a broad array of standards and organizes them into teachable chunks of instructional time. This step helps teams transition into the process of designing instructional units. Next, let's examine a backward process for designing quality instructional units that embeds aligned common formative assessments.

Backward Planning of Specific Units

Backward planning is nothing new. Stephen Covey (2004) has been advocating that effective planning begins with "the end in mind" for quite some time now. Educators Grant Wiggins and Jay McTighe (2005) outline a specific process for the backward design and planning of quality instruction. In their model, they remind educators that before beginning to plan instruction, teachers should identify the type of evidence they will accept in order to confirm that students attained a true understanding of the knowledge and concepts being taught.

We put our own spin on the backward planning model to show how teams can collaboratively determine the focus of their instruction, including the inclusion of aligned common formative assessments. Following are suggested steps in the process.

Step One: Specify and Clarify the Desired Results

In chapter 3, we learned about the process of identifying the power standards for each unit of instruction. This process involves identifying the big ideas and guiding questions that will facilitate and steer student learning throughout the unit. We strongly recommend that teams take the time to translate these standards into student-friendly language, or work in collaboration with their students to rewrite them as part of the instructional process.

Step Two: Unwrap the Standards to Identify the Essential Learning Targets, Context, and Vocabulary

In chapter 4, we learned how to identify what we specifically want students to know and be able to do (the essential learning) and what academic language and vocabulary we want to explicitly teach and monitor for understanding.

Step Three: Identify Acceptable Evidence (Formative and Summative Assessments)

In chapter 5, we discussed defining the evidence of learning that you will expect students to show as a result of your instruction. As a team, you determined what information formative and summative assessments could provide concerning student mastery of essential learning targets along the way and if students have met learning targets at the end of instruction.

Step Four: Create a Sequential Plan for Unit Design

The plan for unit design provides a framework for teams to plan appropriate instruction to achieve the essential targets as well as the integration of common formative assessments. In this part of the process, teams can work collaboratively to proactively identify best practice for instruction, plan out the time frame for implementing common assessments already identified for specific learning targets, and build in time to provide students with additional time and support. Through the creation of this plan, teams will answer the following questions:

- What is the order of our instruction, and what specific targets will we address?
- What instructional activities will support high levels of learning for these targets?
- When will we deliver common formative assessments?
- When will we provide feedback and corrective instruction to students?
- When will we integrate our summative measures?

The Backward Planning Unit Design Template, on page 110 of the Tools for Teams appendix, outlines how teams can use this four-step process of backward planning to design a unit. Figure 6.3 shows a completed sample of the template using a standard from sixth-grade English language arts (Common Core State Standards Initiative, 2010b, pp. 36–44).

Step one: Specify and clarify the desired results.
What power standard(s) will be addressed within this unit?
• Cite textual evidence to support analysis of what the text says explicitly as well as inferences drawn from the text.
• Gather relevant information from multiple print and digital sources; assess the credibility of each source; and quote or paraphrase the data and conclusions of others while avoiding plagiarism and providing basic bibliographic information for sources.
• Integrate information presented in different media or formats (for example, visually, quantitatively) as well as in words to develop a coherent understanding of a topic or issue.
Student-friendly version of the power standards: I will be able to gather information from a number of sources that support a point of view, summarize that information in my own words, and teach others about that information in a media format of my choosing.
What big ideas will be established within this unit?
• Not all sources of information are credible.
• Information is considered more credible when the author has referenced other experts and provides sufficient evidence to support a viewpoint.
• Writers use a number of strategies, including figurative language, inferences, and technical language to help readers understand new concepts or convince them of certain points of view.
What essential questions will guide the learning?
• How do we check the credibility of information that we get from different sources?
• What types of writing strategies support an author's goal to build the reader's understanding of new information?

Figure 6.3: Completed example of a Backward Planning Unit Design Template.

Continued →

Steps two and three: Unwrap the standards to identify the essential learning targets, context, and vocabulary to determine acceptable evidence (formative and summative assessments).		
Students Will Know . . . (What concepts and vocabulary support the standard?)	**Formative Measures** (How will we monitor student progress on these concepts and skills along the way?)	**Summative Measure(s)** (What culminating measure will we use to determine students' overall attainment of this concept?)
Indicators of credible sources Basic Internet domain association and potential implications (credibility)	F.1. Provide students with a list of sources, including web domains, and ask them to rank these on a three-point credibility scale: 1: Probably not credible 2: Would want to confirm using other sources 3: Probably credible	Include *credible sources* within the scoring rubric for final presentation. S.1
Concept of supporting evidence within a text	F.2. Contrast weak evidence with strong evidence (using a T chart).	Include *evidential support* within the scoring rubric for final presentation. S.1
Elements of a quality summary, including parameters related to plagiarism	F.3. Quick write ("ticket out the door")—Outline elements of a quality summary.	Include *effective summarization* within scoring rubric for final presentation. S.1
Vocabulary: Evidence, credible, inference, plagiarism, viewpoint; check vocabulary frames.*		
And Be Able to . . . (What things should students be able to do as part of the standard?)	**Formative Measures** (How will we monitor student progress on these skills along the way? Are there strong and weak models we can provide to students?)	**Summative Measure(s)** (What culminating measure will we use to determine students' overall achievement of this skill?)
Find evidential support within text for author's argument or information.	F.4. Student uses graphic organizer to identify evidential support for the point of view he or she will be restating in his or her presentation.	Include evidential support within scoring rubric for final presentation. S.1
Discriminate credible from noncredible sources of information.	F.5. Student provides an initial list of credible sources used for his or her presentation.	Include *credible sources* within scoring rubric for final presentation. S.1
Summarize multiple sources of information and integrate into a presentation.	F.6. Student outlines key points of good summary (ticket out the door).	Include *effective summarization* within scoring rubric for final presentation. S.1
Design/deliver a presentation or media project that informs the reader or listener about key points and includes evidential support.	F.7. Student creates a timeline for planning and a story map in preparation for his or her presentation.	Include *effective presentation* within scoring rubric for final presentation. S.1

Step four: Create a sequential plan for unit design.		
Dates	Lessons/Activities	Embedded Assessment Checkpoints (Formative and Summative)
Day one of instruction	Hook students into the concept of inaccurate and accurate information with urban myths. Discuss indicators of credible sources, including Internet domains. Have students work in teams to generate characteristics of credible versus noncredible sources of information. Discuss goals for the unit, including "I can" statements.	F.1
Days two and three	Provide explicit instruction on key words and have students create vocabulary frames* for the following terms: evidence, credible, inference, plagiarism, and viewpoint.	Check vocabulary frames
Day four	Provide students with an argument that is an unsupported assertion, and then contrast it with another argument that supports the inference in textual evidence. Draw out the difference between the two.	F.2
Days five and six	Describe the requirements of the project, including the scoring rubric and timeline. Map out the research and development sequence for students. Have students complete their backward plan from the due date, assigning themselves deadlines for each chunk of the process. Have students share their plan with a partner for feedback.	F.7
Days seven and eight	Provide time for students to begin seeking sources to support their selected point of view. Students should submit sources to teacher for a credibility check prior to moving on.	F.5
Days nine and ten	Students engage in gathering information in support of their selected point of view. Students should complete graphic organizer of key points and evidence along the way, which teacher will check prior to beginning presentation.	F.4
Day ten	Review features of effective summaries.	F.3
Days eleven and twelve	Students write draft summaries of their information and submit them for approval.	F.6
Day thirteen	Students "talk through" their presentations with critical friends and make adjustments based on their feedback, using scoring rubrics as a basis for checking the quality.	
Days fourteen and fifteen	Students give presentations.	S.1

*Vocabulary frames help students organize information about terms and concepts. Vocabulary frames typically include the following: description of the word (may include a nonexample), a diagram or illustration, the term, a synonym, and the term used in a sentence.

Designing Instruction for 21st Century Skills

As educators continue to shift to a focus on 21st century skills, which are integrated within the Common Core State Standards, we see a far more complex picture of what students should know and be able to do. Not only do we expect students to know certain content information and be able to demonstrate certain essential skills in the traditional core subjects, but we also expect them to apply knowledge from new areas of learning. These areas include 21st century interdisciplinary themes; life and career skills; learning and innovation skills; and information, media, and technology skills. These areas describe the skills, knowledge, and expertise students must master to succeed in work and life (see table 6.1, page 72; Partnership for 21st Century Skills, 2009).

Table 6.1: 21st Century Skills

21st Century Interdisciplinary Themes	
• Global awareness • Financial, economic, business, and entrepreneurial literacy • Civic literacy	• Health literacy • Environmental literacy
Life and Career Skills	
• Flexibility and adaptability • Initiative and self-direction • Social and cross-cultural skills	• Productivity and accountability • Leadership and responsibility
Learning and Innovation Skills	
• Creativity and innovation • Critical thinking and problem solving	• Communication and collaboration
Information, Media, and Technology Skills	
• Information literacy • Media literacy	• ICT (Information and Communications Technologies) literacy

Source: Partnership for 21st Century Skills, 2009.

As we plan on a big-picture scale, we must address those additional skill layers and contexts in which students demonstrate their learning. A number of resources are currently in development to assist schools and teams in this process. One of the most bountiful resources is the Partnership for 21st Century Skills (www.p21.org). It offers examples of how educators can assess student learning in these new skills and concepts.

Final Thoughts

It is important to remember that your teams will not create these products overnight—some units take time and conversation among team members before they are considered finished. However, teams should not wait until every aspect is perfect before moving forward. When designing units, think about the process as one involving layers of refinement. Each unit you design will be better than the last, in part because the team will be more experienced with the process and thus become far more efficient. Likewise, each time your team teaches the unit (the following year), you will likely refine and improve the plan, such as by revising the scoring rubric or realigning your assessments.

The next chapter will guide your team to one of the biggest payoffs that comes from the common formative assessment process: looking at results and determining, Now what?

CHAPTER 7

Now What?
Using Data to Make a Difference

- The most important result of using common formative assessments is the response teams develop and implement to support student learning.

- In a common formative assessment, data must be gathered *by learning target* for each student.

- Data conversations can follow a prescriptive protocol that allows teams to make effective use of their time and create a safe place to share ideas and information.

While they offer many benefits, the primary goal of common formative assessments is to provide information about student learning and to identify which students are in need of additional time and support. In fact, they are an integral part of a school's Tier 1 instruction within the response to intervention model (Buffum, Mattos, & Weber, 2009). Specifically, in schools that operate as PLCs, teams use the results of their common formative assessments to identify students who have not reached proficiency on prioritized learning targets. What differentiates teams in PLCs from traditional teams is the response itself. In PLCs, when students are identified as not yet reaching proficiency on the skills and concepts considered essential, there is a collective and systematic first response *within the team* designed to provide immediate support. This differs greatly from traditional teams in which members feel it isn't their responsibility to provide support. These teams respond to student needs simply by looking for other teachers or staff, such as specialists, to provide the intervention students need.

In addition, many teams get stuck when examining data and planning a response. They get stuck because they are trying to use a process to analyze their data that is cumbersome and time consuming. For example, many data-analysis protocols ask teachers to first look for facts, then create a hypothesis, and so on. Teachers are taught to look for patterns in their data by graphing their results over time. While these processes are effective when examining summative data, they are less likely to help teams use common formative assessment data effectively.

Mike Schmoker (2003) reminds us that we don't need "sophisticated data analysis or special expertise" (p. 23) to collect and use the data we need. The step-by-step process we describe in this chapter will help your team make decisions about student learning and plan intervention based on meaningful and timely data—your common formative assessments. This process allows teams to plan these next steps in a way that will be practical and will make a difference for students. The Tools for Teams appendix contains two tools to help teams plan as they progress through this process: the Data Team Meeting Template (page 112) provides several graphic organizers for teams to use when bringing their data to the table, and the Protocol for Data Team Meeting document (page 115) highlights the steps in the process.

Step One: Gathering the Data

In chapter 5, your team was encouraged to design formative assessments around a small number of learning targets. You created an assessment plan listing the specific types of questions you would ask and how many you would ask for each of the targets being assessed. So when gathering the data from the assessment, your team should first list the item numbers from the assessment that were written for each learning target. For example, questions one to four were written to assess learning target one, questions five to eight to assess learning target two, and questions nine and ten to assess learning target three.

For example, the seventh-grade math team at Washington Middle School developed a common formative assessment to determine which students understood adding integers. Its assessment plan is shown in figure 7.1.

Learning Targets	Knowledge	Application	Analysis	Evaluation	Total Items/Total Time
T.1: Add negative integers		Four multiple-choice questions (one through four)			Four (six minutes)
T.2: Subtract negative integers		Four multiple-choice questions (five through eight)			Four (six minutes)
T.3: Apply to problem		Two constructed-response questions (nine and ten)			Two (eight minutes)

Figure 7.1: Seventh-grade assessment plan for integers.

To make things simple, the team wrote its assessment so that questions one through four assessed target one, questions five through eight assessed target two, and questions nine and ten assessed target three. Members decided that students would have to get three out of four questions correct to be proficient on targets one and two, and students would have to score a three on a four-point rubric for each of the questions in target three.

At the data team meeting, team members brought with them a list—by learning target—of which students have not reached proficiency, which have reached proficiency but would benefit from additional practice, and which students are beyond proficiency and would benefit from enrichment. This allowed the team to determine the total number of students in need for each level of intervention or enrichment.

In our example of the math team, each of the teachers brought his or her collected data in a form similar to the one in figure 7.2.

Learning Target One: Add Negative Integers		
Needs Time and Support	**Perhaps More Practice**	**Ready for Enrichment**
Sally	Matthew	Aaron
Mary	Jeremy	Andrew
Josh	Samantha	Max
Jennifer	Erin	Cindy
Learning Target Two: Subtract Negative Integers		
Needs Time and Support	**Perhaps More Practice**	**Ready for Enrichment**
Sally	Jennifer	Aaron
Jeremy	Mary	Andrew
Josh	Samantha	Max
Matthew	Erin	Cindy
Learning Target Three: Apply to Problem		
Needs Time and Support	**Perhaps More Practice**	**Ready for Enrichment**
Sally	Josh	Max
Mary	Jeremy	Cindy
Matthew	Aaron	Erin
Jennifer	Andrew	Samantha

Figure 7.2: Sample of collected assessment data for three learning targets.

Step Two: Analyzing the Data

Teams often want to begin planning their next steps for instruction right away when they first meet to look at the data. However, your team will be able to develop a better response plan by taking several initial steps. First, review the proficiency level you established for each learning target to determine if it was set at the appropriate level. For example, in the Washington Middle School example, the team reviewed whether or not level three on the constructed-response rubric represented an appropriate proficiency level for that learning target. Team members also looked to see if any of the multiple-choice questions appeared to be of concern. Sometimes most students who appear to understand the information (based on how they answered other questions for a particular learning target) answer the same question incorrectly. Other times students who appear not to understand a learning target get a particular question correct. Teachers may infer from this observation that a question was not well written. Your team should make note of any problematic questions under the heading "Which questions need to be reviewed?" on page 114 of the Data Team Meeting Template in the Tools for Teams appendix.

Once you note any assessment items that need additional review, your team can begin to analyze the data. Start by listing each learning target and the total number of students who scored below proficiency, met proficiency, and exceeded proficiency. During this step, focus on determining the total number of students who will need additional time and support—not on how that support will happen.

Sometimes schools and districts purchase computer software that score selected-response questions and generate reports with the data by student and learning target. If not, teams can create their own spreadsheets that allow them to sort the data from a formative assessment by learning target (table 7.1).

Table 7.1: Data Sorted by Learning Target

	Learning Target One Proficiency: ¾ or 75%	Learning Target Two Proficiency: ¾ or 75%	Learning Target Three Proficiency: ¾ or 75%
John	75%	75%	3
Jeremy	100%	75%	4
Caitlin	50%	100%	2
Missy	75%	100%	4
Jason	100%	100%	3
Brian	75%	25%	2
Sarah	50%	75%	4

As you discuss your results, you can re-sort for each learning target to see which students scored at each level.

After looking at the total number of students at each level, consider some more general results. Did the same students seem to miss all of the learning targets? Is the number of students who need additional help only a small percentage of the total number of students, or is there a larger majority who didn't understand a target? The answers to these questions will help your team decide whether or not additional whole-class instruction is needed around a learning target, or if teachers can respond to students in smaller groups.

Step Three: Planning the Response

Once your team knows the total number of students in need of additional time and support for each learning target, you can begin to plan how to respond. To do this, you must further analyze the results of the assessment. The following questions will help your team effectively uncover a plan to respond to the data.

Which Teacher Was Most Effective?

Your team might recognize that one teacher was more successful on a particular learning target than the rest of the team. One of the benefits of common assessments is that teams can compare their results to the results of their colleagues. In fact, according to DuFour et al. (2010a), each teacher needs to see the data for his or her students "*in comparison to other students* in the school attempting to meet that same standard" (p. 189). They remind us that "without relevant information on their respective strengths and weaknesses, teacher conversations regarding the most effective ways to help students learn a concept will deteriorate into sharing of uninformed opinions—'This is how I like to teach it'" (DuFour et al., 2008, p. 27).

A teacher who was more successful at teaching a particular learning target can share his or her instructional strategies with the group, and the team might decide that students who need more time and support should be assigned to that teacher to receive further support on that target.

What Mistakes Did Students Make?

Your team might also discover when analyzing data that each teacher has roughly the same number of students who experienced difficulty on a learning target. In this case, using one teacher's instructional strategy for additional support is not necessarily the answer. Instead, create a hypothesis as to why students experienced difficulty in understanding the target. This will help plan how you will support students with additional instruction.

Start by listing possible reasons why you think students experienced difficulty. Teachers might, for example, notice that the students who experienced difficulty appear to have weak background knowledge or prerequisite skills. They know that these students will need additional scaffolding and reinforcement of background knowledge to learn the target. Teachers might also hypothesize that students had difficulty because the target is an abstract concept, thus students will benefit from more concrete learning opportunities around this target. Teachers might discover that certain students have a common misconception that is getting in the way of their understanding of a learning target, so students will need help to overcome their misconception.

For example, the physics team at Harbour View High School gave its students an assessment asking them to analyze some graphs from an experiment and then develop and explain a conclusion drawn from the information. The team members used eight multiple-choice questions and two constructed-response questions on their assessment. As they looked at their results, they discovered that a number of students got all of the multiple-choice questions correct, but missed the constructed-response questions asking them to develop a conclusion. The team hypothesized that these students really did understand how to analyze information from a graph, but they didn't know how to develop a coherent conclusion *in writing*. By creating hypotheses about why students didn't learn a particular target, a team builds possible ways to respond with corrective instruction.

In chapter 5, we discussed that some teams write their multiple-choice questions with specific distracters to know what mistakes their students are making. If your team wrote questions this way, it will be important at this step to look at the item analysis to see which students made which mistakes. For example, if the multiple-choice question has four choices (one correct and three based on common misunderstandings students have), you can know more specifically why students got it wrong.

Since the purpose of formative assessment is to know exactly which students haven't learned a particular target and *what we need to do next for them,* it's important to use the data from our assessments in an unbiased way. However, while teachers need to be open-minded about why students are experiencing difficulty learning a particular target, it is important that they use their knowledge about students to create a meaningful hypothesis about why students didn't learn the target. This prevents us from using the "they just didn't even try" excuse for students who regularly experience difficulty meeting proficiency.

How Can We Provide Corrective Instruction?

Once teachers brainstorm their hypotheses, they then turn to plans for providing corrective instruction based on why they think students did not reach proficiency. In the example from the Washington Middle School math team, the team discovered that subtracting negative integers is a concept with which many of its students had difficulty. Knowing that this is a highly abstract concept, members hypothesized that students really didn't understand the abstraction. Therefore, they planned to reteach the concept using manipulatives to make it more concrete.

One teacher shared a strategy using chips with different colors on each side. The red side represents a negative number and the yellow side a positive number. In the math problem $3 - (-2) = x$, the student lays out three yellow chips to represent the first number in the problem. He then adds two yellow chips and two red chips because together they equal zero. (The student knows that you can add zero without affecting the outcome.) Then the student removes two red chips (representing that he has subtracted a negative two). The final solution is five because the student has five chips remaining. The teacher then reviews the rules for subtracting negative numbers to demonstrate that the subtraction sign and the negative sign cancel each other out so that the final sum is the addition of the two numbers.

In the earlier example of the high school physics team, the team responded to the students who got the multiple-choice questions correct and the constructed-response questions incorrect by helping students learn how to develop a strong paragraph in writing explaining their conclusion.

What Other Resources Do We Have for Support?

Sometimes after examining data, a team realizes that no teachers used a highly effective teaching strategy for a particular learning target, and the team can't explain why its students didn't do very well. In this case, the team members decide that their next step should be to go back into best-practice research to see what additional strategies they might want to consider. For example, Marzano, Pickering, and Pollock (2001) describe nine highly effective, research-based strategies to help students:

1. Identifying similarities and differences

2. Summarizing and note taking

3. Reinforcing effort and providing recognition

4. Homework and practice

5. Nonlinguistic representations

6. Cooperative learning

7. Setting objectives and providing feedback

8. Generating and testing hypotheses

9. Cues, questions, and advanced organizers

Teams can choose one strategy to use in their intervention efforts with students who didn't reach proficiency. Reviewing the professional literature to determine the most current thinking about best practice will help the team build a repertoire of strategies that it can use to teach a concept or learning target. The original strategy team members used in their classrooms might still work for the majority of students, but it hasn't worked for all students. This step asks teams to consider additional strategies beyond their team.

Step Four: Reviewing the Assessment

Your team should also review the assessment as a whole so you can discuss whether or not you want to use the same assessment items in the future. Look back at the questions you identified as in need of review. Some questions might just need to be reworded because they are not clear enough, and others, such as constructed-response items, might need a clearer context. You might decide that some of your items weren't written at a high enough level to assess the thinking your instruction was designed to target. Your team should also discuss how long it took for students to take the assessment, and how long it took you to score their responses. Finally, your team should discuss instructional and pacing issues it might want to adjust in the future.

Consider, for example, the sixth-grade English language arts team at Meadowview Middle School. Members realized during their data meeting about an assessment on sentence structure that the questions they were asking were primarily factual questions and that students already knew the material they were assessing. The teachers realized that instead of asking questions about types of sentences, they would get better information if they asked students to take a piece of writing and edit it to show how to use a variety of sentence structures (combining sentences and varying sentence length).

Or consider the biology team members at Jefferson High School who realized after their assessment that the majority of their students were still having difficulty understanding the difference between *diffusion* and *osmosis*. They agreed to spend two more days of instruction and use several additional activities. They noted this on their pacing guide so they would be sure to do the same the following year.

At Earhart Elementary School, the third-grade team members questioned the time it was taking to administer their reading assessments. After much discussion, they decided that they were trying to assess too many learning targets every time they did a formative assessment as they were trying to assess some vocabulary and some strategies, as well as including some writing targets. Instead, they agreed that they would assess one or two skills only—such as finding the main idea and details—and that they would base their questions on one reading passage.

Your team should also review the consistency of your scoring practices in this step. When a team uses a rubric to score student work products or performances, it is important that all teachers apply the same criteria to those products and performances. To test whether or not teachers are applying the same criteria, teams can do the following exercise: Each teacher brings three or four random samples of student work to the group. Each teacher then scores each sample and puts his or her score in a private location (on a scoring sheet that isn't passed along with the sample, on a sticky note placed on the back of the sample, and so on). Once each teacher has scored all the work samples, the team looks at the range of scores given to that piece of work. If the scores are all within a point or two (depending on the number of points on the rubric), then the team can assume individual members are applying the rubric equally. However, if the sample has a range greater than one or two points, it is important for the team to discuss the disparate score to come to consensus on the appropriate mark. This process not only validates the scoring for the work samples brought to the meeting but for the rest of the student work as well.

Another process some teams use to ensure consistency is to score all of the work together at their meeting. In this case, teachers exchange work samples so that they're not scoring the work done by their own students. Before they begin the scoring process, the teachers examine several anchor papers that represent the quality of work for each level of the rubric.

Step Five: Next Steps

Once you have analyzed your data, you will develop a plan for your team's next steps. You have shared ideas about the best instructional strategies for intervention and how you will respond to students who have not learned. Now you need to decide who will deliver those corrective instructional strategies and to which of your students. This begins with finding the time.

Finding Time to Respond

Often the decision about how to respond is dependent on the school's master schedule or a team's schedule. In this next section, we'll look at some specific ways schools and teams have reworked their schedules to find time to respond.

Elementary Teams

Many elementary schools create their master schedules to provide common teaching time for all teachers at a particular grade level. This time might be called *walk-to time*, *intervention time*, or even just *the literacy or math block*. What's important about this common teaching time is that all teachers on the team share their students, so that teachers can move students into different classrooms depending on students' specific needs. During this time, all of the teachers are working with groups of students to respond to assessment data, whether to support learning needs, practice, or enrich. None of the teachers is providing new instruction during this time, so none of the students misses any important initial instruction, which would put him or her even further behind.

For example, at Jackson Elementary, three first-grade team members just finished their instruction about how to tell time to the nearest half hour using an analog clock. They used a short formative assessment to determine that approximately 20 percent of their students will need some corrective instruction before the class can move on to the next lesson in the unit. During its data meeting, the team created a plan to spend an additional two days to make sure that all students learned this important learning target. Teachers decided to divide their students into three groups, with each teacher responsible for one group.

One teacher will work with students who need corrective instruction using a strategy the team members developed during their data meeting based on why they think the students didn't learn the target. A second teacher will take a group of students who passed the assessment but will benefit from some additional practice. The third teacher will take the students who know the target and will benefit from enrichment. The students who didn't learn the target will also be given another assessment to make sure they've learned it after receiving additional support. This assessment can be a different formative assessment that assesses the same target, or it might even be the same assessment given earlier. If there are students who still need additional help after this second assessment, the team will plan a Tier 2 intervention for this small group.

Sometimes elementary teams add additional staff to help keep their student groups smaller. For example, at Skyview Elementary, the first-grade team planned a response similar to that of Jackson

Elementary, except it has a math specialist and an instructional aide available during the scheduled math time. By adding these two staff members, the team is able to create two smaller groups of students from those who need corrective instruction: one taught by a classroom teacher and one by the math specialist. The rest of the students are divided between the two remaining teachers and the instructional aide for additional practice (taught by one of the teachers and the instructional assistant) and for extension activities (taught by the third teacher).

Secondary Teams

Middle and high school teams often have more difficulty finding time for corrective instruction because their master schedules are so complex. However, there are still a number of ways schools can find the time they need—they just need to be creative. For example, one high school we've worked with developed its master schedule so that every time one of its core ninth-grade classes meets, there is at least one other section of the same core class meeting at that same time. In other words, if Algebra I is taught during first period, there are at least two sections meeting first period. This allows those two teachers to exchange students after formative assessment to provide intervention and enrichment.

Many middle schools have two or more teams at each grade level, so their master schedules make it possible for teachers to exchange students between the teams when responding to formative assessments. One caution we make is that when teachers exchange students, they do so for a day or two only at one time based on the results of a formative assessment; they should not group students permanently or for a long period of time. This flexible grouping will support specific learning needs without exposing less-able students to the negative outcomes of grouping them into a "low group."

In addition, many middle and high schools are creating master schedules that have a built-in intervention period either daily or several days a week. For example, if the school has an eight-period day, a few minutes are shaved off each period to create a half-hour period during the day when all students are available for intervention or enrichment. Then the team can organize the students who need more time and support into smaller groups. Students who already learned the target receive enrichment during this time.

Finally, some high schools have resource rooms for students to use during their study halls. If a student is identified as not having reached proficiency on a particular learning target, he or she can go to the resource room to get help from a staff member who is not assigned to be teaching at that time.

Designing Tier 2 Response

No matter what structure your team uses to provide time for response, the most important thing is that there is a response and a follow-up assessment for any learning target a student missed. Teams must decide when to give follow-up assessments and what they will look like. As we mentioned, some teams choose to use a different version of the first formative assessment; others use the exact same assessment. The critical issue is that teams measure whether or not students have mastered the target after the intervention.

So what happens when students still haven't mastered an important learning target after the initial instruction, formative assessment, and corrective instruction? What happens when a student takes the end-of-unit test and doesn't show proficiency on one or more essential standards? Even when the initial core instruction is over, teams within PLCs don't abandon students who haven't yet mastered essential learning outcomes. In a PLC where the school has developed a tiered system of response—a pyramid of interventions—there are many ways students can receive more time and support to learn beyond the core instruction. These are known as Tier 2 and Tier 3 responses. These additional learning opportunities are provided to the smaller number of students who need even more support, and often happen in addition to new instruction in the classroom. For example, in an elementary school where a student received initial instruction on a reading concept, was identified through a formative assessment as needing extra help, was provided with correction instruction, and then was identified in a follow-up assessment as still not having mastered the target, the student is given more intensive smaller group intervention. He or she may be pulled out for small-group instruction or a specialist might "push in" to the classroom. Either way, the student continues to get instruction and support on the essential outcomes that are most important for learning. Visit "Evidence of Effectiveness" at www.allthingsplc.info for more examples of schoolwide systems of intervention and enrichment.

Creating Safe Conditions for Teams

When teams examine the results of common formative assessments together, it is important that team members create a safe environment for one another. However, as Wellman and Lipton (2004) point out, "safety and comfort is not always the same thing in collaborative settings" (p. 12) and teams must work on developing trust around their use of data. If you never discussed your team norms for behavior concerning the use of data, you might find you need to revisit this process after your first assessment or two. Norms should include the understanding that teams will treat the information from their assessments objectively. Teams shouldn't be judgmental—rather, members should examine data and state facts so that they can create accurate hypotheses about why students struggled (Steele & Boudett, 2008).

The Best Hopes/Worst Fears activity (Wellman & Lipton, 2004) is one way for teams to establish a trusting environment. In this activity, members brainstorm on a T chart their best hopes and worst fears about using common formative assessments. Team members often acknowledge that they are afraid their colleagues will be judgmental, that their results will not be as positive as they had hoped, that they will look bad to their teammates, and so on. Once these concerns are out on the table, your team can address each of them by creating data norms, such as the following:

- We will look for facts, not blame.

- We will learn from the results of our assessments.

- We will not judge our colleagues.

Once you've discussed your fears, remind yourselves about why this work is so important—what are your best hopes? These hopes will likely include higher student success, more personal satisfaction, increased knowledge of instructional strategies, and various other learning outcomes. You'll likely conclude that the benefits of common formative assessments outweigh the possible fears.

Final Thoughts

It is critical for teachers to know what their students are learning and not learning so they can make decisions about instruction. By doing data analysis together, your team will be able to provide much stronger and more successful intervention and enrichment, as well as gain valuable professional development for all members. But remember, the best data analysis leads to action by the team—otherwise students will not benefit.

CHAPTER 8

Getting the Most Bang for Your Assessment Buck— Involving Students

KEY POINTS

- Students are important users of assessment information.

- By including students in the assessment process, the responsibility for learning will ultimately shift from the teacher to the student.

- Research supports that when students are a part of the assessment process, they learn at higher rates.

Too often, educators believe that assessment is one sided—that it is what teachers do *to* students to determine what they have learned and are able to do. This may even be true for teams implementing common formative assessments: they design and use the assessments, collectively examine the data, determine what actions to take based on the results, and take those actions. In this chapter, we expand the concept of formative assessment to include students and detail how their deeper involvement can actually improve their learning. Consider the following scenario.

The sixth-grade social studies team at Foster Middle School is just beginning its unit on the early civilization of China. The team agrees in advance on the essential learning targets for the unit:

- Students will be able to describe the geographic features of China that made governance and the spread of ideas and goods difficult and served to isolate the country from the rest of the world; and

- Discuss the political and cultural problems prevalent in the time of Confucius and how he sought to solve them. (California State Board of Education, 1998, p. 26)

After a hook activity in which teachers provide a pictorial sequence of both traditional and modern-day life in China, teachers share and discuss the learning targets with their students. This discussion outlines what students will know and do by the end of the unit and explains that students will demonstrate their learning by developing a graphic organizer that describes how traditions, beliefs, and geographic location influenced daily life in China during early civilization. Additionally, students will develop an essay that discusses the influence and potential frustrations of Confucius, and parallels issues he faced during that time with ones he might face today. These targets are tied to a larger big idea about the concepts of global economy and a shrinking world. Students record "I can" statements in their learning notebooks, such as the following: "I can describe the political and cultural issues that China faced long ago and compare those issues with China today."

Throughout instruction, teachers administer common formative assessments that gauge student understanding of concepts and information. Following each common formative assessment, students receive immediate feedback on where they stand with the learning targets. They then construct a plan for how they will move forward, using the feedback as a guide for improvement. Embedded within the unit instruction are minilessons in which students engage in a scaffolded process of developing their written essay, spending time on key indicators and examining the indicators of quality based on a teacher-made rubric. Students have the opportunity to examine anchor papers and are guided in a discussion about the quality indicators of those products. Peers serve as "critical friends" to review the writing of their fellow students and provide specific feedback before students turn in their final essays.

The students in this classroom are clear about their status with proficiency of learning targets, and they know what the desired level of quality looks like. They are highly involved in the assessment process, and it's likely that their learning is greater than if they had not been a part of the process. A key element of their involvement is formative assessment.

James Popham's (2008b) definition of formative assessment—"a *planned process* in which assessment-elicited *evidence* of students' status is used by teachers to *adjust their ongoing instructional practices or* by *students* to adjust their current learning tactics" (p. 6, italics added)—reinforces what numerous studies have demonstrated (Black & Wiliam, 1998): students play a key role in the assessment process.

Popham also provides a hierarchy of assessment implementation as a guide for schools examining their practices in assessment. He defines a Level 1 classroom as one in which the teacher is making instructional adjustments based on the results of student assessment. We know that there is great power in this practice. However, we would challenge teams to examine the next level in Popham's hierarchy: Level 2. At this level, students use results to adjust their learning strategies. Students are engaged in the process from beginning to end. They are clear on what they're learning, and through a process of engagement in the feedback, they are clear on where they need to go next. In our experience in and observations of many classrooms, assessment practices implemented at this level result in an exponential boost in student learning. When teachers implement this practice of involving students for every student in the classroom, they reach the next level—Level 3, the classroom climate shift. This shift is best described as a change from students focusing only on grades to a true focus on their learning. Figure 8.1 shows this powerful shift.

But to say that there is a shift in the ownership of learning is not descriptive enough. What's most critical is that students begin to understand that they are in control and empowered to change the course of their learning—in other words, they become more responsible and able to respond. Students are no longer being "done to" by the teacher; they are actually working in partnership with the teacher to learn at higher levels.

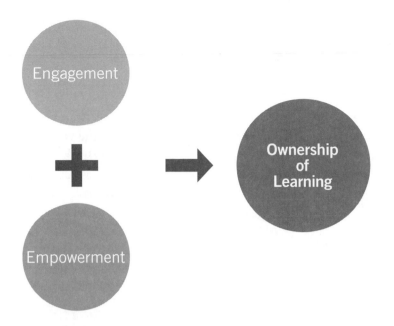

Figure 8.1: The shift in student focus from grades to a true focus on learning.

When teams use common formative assessments effectively *and* involve students in the process, they reach Level 4 in Popham's model: attaining schoolwide implementation. When teams are truly engaged in the common formative assessment process, they examine the practices that are most successful across the team, and they work to adjust their practices collectively so that all students learn at high levels. By involving the most important users of assessment information—students—teams help students to become responsible for their own learning, which goes beyond the single classroom. Teams are now working together to impact the schoolwide system.

If your team wants to become partners with your students to make the most of the assessment process, we highly recommend the following practices.

Help Students Know What They Will Learn and Why

In chapter 4, we discussed how the unwrapping process serves to reveal specific learning targets contained within the standards. As a result of participating in the unwrapping process, all members of a grade-level or course team gain clarity on what students should know and be able to do, so they are more likely to align their instruction and assessment. That same clarity is essential for students. Students need to know what they will be learning and why. Paul Black and Dylan Wiliam (2007) share that students can achieve a learning goal only if they understand that goal and can assess what they need to do to reach it. Simply writing a standard on the board, a popular practice in many schools, won't necessarily provide a clear picture of what students are expected to know or do, or the reasons why.

How do we communicate clear targets to students? If our goal is that they reference them and use those targets as a guide for their own learning, targets must be written in student-friendly language. Now this is not to say that we should eliminate all academic words. Rather, we must make sure that students understand what those words mean. Additionally, we want students to have ownership of the learning targets. To that end, several experts (Marzano, 2006; Stiggins et al., 2004) suggest that targets be written in a particular way. Stiggins suggests using "I can" or "I will be able to" stems for learning targets. For example, instead of "Students will add and subtract fractions with different denominators," we might use the statement, "I will be able to use equivalent fractions as a strategy to add and subtract fractions." This statement not only describes what students will be able to do after instruction but also how the learning will be helpful to them.

To increase student connectedness to the learning targets, teachers can also write targets so that they identify how students will demonstrate their skill or knowledge and the value of that skill or knowledge: for example, "I will be able to use figurative language and will show this by orally describing a setting in a way that is interesting for the reader." Students are clear not only on what they will be learning but also how and why it's important. This practice helps students achieve a clear view of what they're working to achieve and why. It helps them to keep the end in mind.

Moss and Brookhart (2009) suggest teachers check student understanding of learning targets by asking them to respond to the following questions: What are you going to learn? Why is this important? Can you connect this learning target to a previous lesson that we've had?

Engage Students in Defining Quality Work

Students also need to understand what it takes to succeed—this shouldn't be a secret held by the teacher alone. Students need a clear picture of the features of quality work—whether it's a well-written essay, an appropriately worded hypothesis, or a well-designed project. Most often, educators are the ones to decide how to categorize or score student work based on its quality. However, it is our opinion, and the opinion of various experts, that students benefit from being engaged in the process of defining quality—of actively participating in making meaning and personal connections with the information, rather than simply being handed a list of features or a rubric. Moss and Brookhart (2009) recommend two key strategies for engaging students in the examination of quality work:

1. **Look at examples**—Ask students to examine quality samples of anonymous work. (You can use the work of students from prior years, but be sure to remove the names.) Ask students to list the features that make them good examples. Groups of students can also sort examples of work on a continuum from weakest to strongest based on key features referenced in teacher-made rubrics, such as the use of supporting details or a well-defined problem statement.

2. **Use rubrics**—Beginning with teacher-made rubrics, ask students to review a sample of work and decide where it might fall on the rubric. Students can initially work in teams to compare work to the rubric. Students can then refine and even put the rubric into their own words to make a personal connection with the information. Gradually, students shift to examining their own work in comparison to the rubric, and then that of their peers.

When teachers and students work together to design rubrics to score common formative assessments, the rubrics themselves become a part of the learning—not just a way to measure learning.

Consider the sample rubric in figure 8.2, which is written around three learning targets identified for the development of a research project. If the teacher gives the student a score of three for learning target A (development of a research question), a four for learning target B (use of appropriate sources of information), and a two for learning target C (organization of content), the student can determine the next steps she must take. Empowered with information within the rubric, she can use the description of each of the three learning targets to improve the quality of her work. When students are engaged in the process of working with the rubric prior to comparing it with their own work, they have a clearer understanding of the expectations and can more easily reflect on what they need to do to improve.

Learning Target	4	3	2	1
A: Development of a research question	Developed well-written research questions that were relevant to the research topic and "hooked" the reader.	Developed specific questions that were appropriate and relevant to the research topic.	Used research questions that were not entirely appropriate or relevant to the research topic.	Did not develop a research question.
B: Use of appropriate sources of information	Used highly appropriate and varied sources of information in support of the research (books, articles, primary sources).	Used appropriate sources of information in support of the research (books, articles, primary sources).	Used limited but appropriate information in support of the research.	No appropriate sources were used in support of this research.
C: Organization of content	Presented information clearly and concisely with a logical progression of ideas and effective supporting evidence.	Presented content with a logical progression of ideas and supporting evidence.	Did not create a consistent focus or effective organization of information, and failed to provide an adequate amount of supporting evidence.	Content was poorly organized and unfocused. Little or no supporting evidence was provided.

Figure 8.2: Sample rubric for student assessment.

Focus on Timely, Effective Feedback and Self-Reporting—Not Grades

As we shared in chapter 2, the focus of common formative assessments is not to determine grades; rather, the focus is on the information they reveal for both teachers and students. John Hattie (2009) states that when he completed the first synthesis after examining thousands of studies on possible influences on achievement, "it soon became clear that feedback was among the most powerful influences on achievement. Most programs and methods that worked best were based on heavy dollops of feedback" (p. 173). In fact, in his meta-analysis of the effectiveness of instructional practices, Hattie (2009) identified students' self-reporting of grades as the most powerful strategy out of 138 instructional practices he examined:

> It was only when I discovered that feedback was most powerful when it is from the student to the teacher that I started to understand it better. When teachers seek, or at least are open to, feedback from students as to what students know, what they understand, where they make errors, when they have misconceptions, when they are not engaged—then teaching and learning can be synchronized and powerful. Feedback to teachers helps make learning visible. (p. 173)

Effective feedback is intentionally delivered to provide students with specific information about what they understand and the areas in which they still need to build proficiency, and to guide them to employ specific strategies they must use to improve. Frequent and specific feedback deepens the conversations around student learning. When students begin to make comparisons between their work and the indicators of quality, they are actually generating the feedback.

In their seminal article "Inside the Black Box," Paul Black and Dylan Wiliam (1998) share their perspective on the power of specific and targeted feedback:

> When anyone is trying to learn, feedback about the effort has three elements: recognition of the desired goal, evidence about present position, and some understanding of a way to close the gap between the two. All three must be understood to some degree by anyone before he or she can take action to improve learning. (p. 143)

In order for feedback to be effective, it must be provided in a timely fashion—in other words, close enough to the learning so students connect it to their most recent learning goal. According to Susan Brookhart (2008), feedback should be provided when students "are still mindful of the topic, assignment, or performance in question. It needs to come while they still think of the learning goal as a learning goal—that is, something they are still striving for, not something they already did" (pp. 10, 11). If the feedback doesn't take place until the gap is too large, or perceived as too large, students may feel overwhelmed with the magnitude of correction or sense that that their efforts will be futile.

We strongly recommend that teams discuss when and how they will share feedback from their common formative assessments with students in a timely fashion and how they might engage students in the process of self-feedback. The goal is to provide feedback that helps students know what's working and what's not, and supporting them as they embark on improvement by giving them specific strategies for getting closer to the target.

Partner With Students to Monitor Their Progress and Communicate Their Strengths and Weaknesses

We've discussed a number of ways to engage students in the assessment process. However, it's essential to embed this engagement into your instruction in a stair-step, or scaffolded, way. A familiar strategy that you most likely use within your instruction is the I do/We do/You do approach. In this approach, the "I do" is the beginning phase in which teachers use minimal-risk strategies, such as modeling and using think-alouds, to show students the steps and thinking behind key processes, such as comparing quality seen in a piece of writing to indicators on a rubric. Students then reflect and comment on their perceptions of the process. In the "We do" stage, the teacher and students perform the process at the same time, a low-risk activity. For example, they might examine student samples of a mathematics problem to determine the types of errors that were made. Then teachers guide students through the process, often in cooperative groups, and students are asked to do a similar activity. Finally, during the "You do" portion of instruction, students apply their newly learned strategy by examining their own work or the work of their peers, a medium-risk activity. Teachers ask guiding questions throughout the process that help to structure the learning.

The goal of the I do/We do/You do approach is to scaffold the release of responsibility for learning by moving from simple to more complex analyses, and working from a nonthreatening context (minimal risk) toward one that focuses on students' own personal work (medium risk). Figure 8.3 outlines this process.

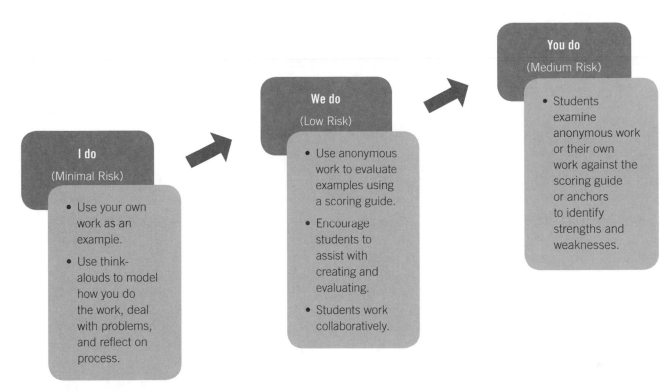

Figure 8.3: The I do/We do/You do process.

The Student-Involved Assessment Worksheet in the Tools for Teams appendix (page 116) will help your team monitor its progress toward student involvement in the assessment process.

Final Thoughts

By bringing students into the assessment process, we accomplish several things:

- We empower them with clear learning targets so that they really know what they're expected to learn and why.

- We help them examine how they're doing in relation to the targets by providing them with specific feedback and a process for analyzing where they stand in relation to the targets.

- We help build their understanding of strategies and quality so that they can arrive at the intended target.

- We see a subtle but clear shift from the teacher being responsible for student learning toward shared responsibility or partnership in learning, in which the student is an actively engaged decision maker who uses feedback and data to plan his or her next steps.

John Hattie (2009) references a model of *visible learning* that he defines as "when teachers see learning through the eyes of the students *and* when students see themselves as their own teachers" (p. 238). In his own words, Hattie shares that he chooses to "work as a coach, not a scorekeeper" (p. 240). By engaging students in the assessment process and being partners in their learning, we are coaching them along their learning journey.

CHAPTER 9

Sustaining the Work

KEY POINTS

- In a PLC, the goal is continuous improvement. Common formative assessments can be the driving force of that improvement.
- Teams can sustain their efforts by continuously focusing on the *why*, examining their results, and celebrating their successes.
- Common formative assessments are best implemented as part of a system—one that informs interventions and teacher practice on a schoolwide basis.

We've had the pleasure of working with teams across the United States as they have developed and used common formative assessments. With few exceptions, two patterns have emerged.

First, when teams collaboratively design, implement, and analyze common formative assessments, their *collective* understanding of what students should know and do greatly increases. Second, when teams use common formative assessments, they shift from *lesson* planning to *learning planning*. Teams are focused on getting the desired results from students and responding accordingly when students are not learning. Teams steeped in the use of common formative assessments don't blame the students—on the contrary, they examine their instructional practices and find solutions for supporting student learning.

To continue their patterns of success, teams using common formative assessments and the processes described in this book must consider several important questions: How do teams keep improving? How do they stay motivated? How do they sustain their efforts?

In this chapter, we'll try to answer these questions by examining a number of factors that help teams sustain success and continue to improve.

Remain Focused on the Why

At times, teams are so closely focused on the product they are creating that they lose sight of why they are doing the work. They want to "get it right" and "check it off the list." They sometimes rush through the conversations about what to measure or the analysis of results because they feel pressure to finish—whether because of external time constraints or a desire to simply clear their plates of the task. This is where understanding the *why* is crucial. Why are we doing common formative assessments?

In *Revisiting Professional Learning Communities at Work*, DuFour et al. (2008) discuss the importance of building a culture in which results drive the decisions schools and teams make. Popham (2008b) also describes such a culture in his discussion of schoolwide implementation of best practices in assessment. We assert that when every team utilizes common formative assessments, and there is a culture of using data to continuously adjust instruction *collectively*, then a school has shifted to that culture of results.

We want teams to continuously remind themselves that the purpose of these meaningful embedded assessments is to inform both teachers and students about where they are in relation to specific learning targets so that *students can learn more*. Ideally, we would like to see this articulated and clarified across every team in a school. This would dispel any misconceptions about how the results might be used. In our experience, we've found that once teachers feel comfortable that data from common formative assessments will be used to help identify students who are experiencing difficulty, and *not* for judging them as professionals, they are more willing to engage in the process.

Reflect on All the Benefits of Using Common Formative Assessments

As teams experience the Plan, Do, Study, Act cycle (described in chapter 1) inherent in the process of using of common formative assessments, they become much more knowledgeable not only about what students are expected to know but about how they can best teach this knowledge. The conversations that take place during the unwrapping process seem to automatically guide teachers toward better instruction. Paired with backward planning of meaningful assessments, it would be difficult *not* to be learning along with your colleagues. Common formative assessments improve student learning, but we must also recognize their power to improve teacher learning and impact instructional practice. We recommend that teams push back their chairs from the table every now and then and reflect on the impact that they have made from an instructional standpoint. In our work, we've had the opportunity to hear many testimonials. One of the most moving, however, was from a veteran teacher who bravely shared the following:

> I've been teaching a long time. I didn't think I could learn anything from my colleagues. But since we've been doing these assessments, and really talking about how the kids are doing and what works, I feel like I'm actually growing again. This is so different from just sitting in a workshop. And I'm seeing that I've got some pretty smart colleagues. It feels good, and I feel like it isn't just a meeting—it's a team.

Provide or Seek Support for Teams

Teams need support to continue to successfully design and implement common formative assessments. Teams must have time to meet to do their work collaboratively. This means that time for collaboration must be built into the contractual school day. The amount of time needed to do this work varies, but we recommend that teams have at least thirty minutes per week. Teams with longer and more frequent common planning time find that they can establish a pattern to their work flow, allowing them to plan and write their assessment during one meeting and analyze the results and plan the response during a second meeting. As a result, these teams often find that they are able to use common formative assessments as often as weekly. If you are in a leadership position, work collaboratively to identify areas in which this time might be found. If you're not in a leadership position, work collaboratively with your administrator in a solution-oriented way. Remember to focus on the why, and you'll be propelled to find the time to meet.

The second thing teams need to carry out this work is time to respond to the assessments they administer. For some teams, the opportunity to provide intervention occurs in the classroom after the assessment, and for other teams, there is a separate intervention time during the school day. When there is an intervention time built into the school day, teachers are able to share students and, thus, they can provide a more targeted response. Leaders communicate their support of the process by facilitating response to assessment by developing a master schedule that allows time for interventions in the school day. We recommend, however, that you don't create a master schedule with intervention time until you are ready to write and use common formative assessments to determine the need for intervention. Schools that restructure their schedules first often find that they have created a period for implementing remedial classes or programs rather than for the immediate response to short formative assessments.

Building a supportive culture for this work involves ensuring that teachers are comfortable using data. Data help you help your students. They are not information for placing blame. To create a supportive culture, it is important that data conversations stay focused on the facts—the student results and planning for response. Some schools and districts have gone so far as to promise teachers that common formative assessment data will not be used to evaluate teachers.

One of the things that leaders can do to emphasize the benefits of a data-rich culture is to make data easily accessible to all teachers. When there is a computer system teams can use to access and manipulate their data to help them understand them, teachers must be trained to use it and have access to it from their desktop or laptop computers. We realize that security issues are important considerations when deciding who can use the data, but if leaders want their teachers to make the quick decisions needed to respond to common formative assessments, it is important that they have access to their data in the most expeditious way.

Build Capacity to Lead the Work

As we've shared consistently within this book, using common formative assessments yields heightened learning for both students and teachers. In a PLC, there is collective ownership of the process, and to that end, the process itself should be guided not by one or two individuals but by teams empowered with the capacity to do the work. Common formative assessments are a perfect vehicle to begin building capacity. In the Plan, Do, Study, Act cycle, teams participate in what researchers consider to be the highest quality of professional development (Newmann & Wehlage, 1995) work that is directly related to students, team based with an emphasis on sharing expertise, and embedded into the school day. Yet for some teams to move forward in these somewhat uncharted territories, they need time to work with or be facilitated by supportive leaders and coaches who can help them be learners. Ideally, a district or school will design and implement a way to support teams as they grow in their ability to guide the work. Once established, it's also critical for teams to go beyond what they view as traditional team leadership. While it's typical to have a grade-level lead teacher or department chair facilitate team meetings, we encourage teams to spread the leadership across all members. Members of the team should each have a role in guiding the work of the team.

Remember That Experience Yields Efficiency

It's essential that team time is spent in a worthwhile fashion. In the beginning of this book, we discussed how teams should establish a work flow wherein their decisions and actions from one meeting are connected to the decisions and actions they make in their next meeting. We believe that this empowers teams to see the meaning behind their work and make connections along the way. It's important to recognize that over time, teams get into a groove with their work, and the Plan, Do, Study, Act cycle shifts from feeling a little stiff or imposed to a natural way of doing business. This is particularly important to remember when teams are just beginning the process—they may feel uncertain or frustrated at the beginning.

In fact, we believe that teams will establish a routine as they plan and implement each unit of instruction. They will also establish a routine for the school year (and beyond) to make a long-term difference in their own learning and in the achievement of their students.

Be Attentive to Both Immediate and Systemic Learning

Used effectively, common formative assessments guide teams to implement an immediate response to the data—timely corrective instruction for students who demonstrate the need for additional time and support. Teams identify learning targets, design an aligned assessment, assess students, and swiftly provide support for students who did not demonstrate proficiency.

What's also very exciting is when teams use common formative assessments to bring about systemic change and improvement, including evaluating and changing long-term expectations for students as a result of the data you are gathering. Our experience is that after a year or two of implementation of common formative assessments, teams find that students are starting to come to them already having learned the targets. When this happens, teams must decide whether they are going to eliminate the duplicated power standard from their lists or whether they will increase the rigor of expectations for student learning. Consider the following example.

The fifth-grade team at Longfellow Elementary School had been working with the Common Core State Standard for English language arts: "Determine the meaning of words and phrases as they are used in a text, including figurative language such as metaphors and similes" (Common Core State Standards Initiative, 2010b, p. 12). For two years in a row, as specified in their pacing guide, team members gave students a preassessment for their understanding of metaphors and similes, and for two years in a row, they found that students were already able to do the standard as written. This team's learning prompted a conversation in which they discussed a need to refine their pacing guide. In addition, the team discussed how it might further use this information to ensure that all students were learning at high levels, even those that already knew the information. The team developed the following options:

- Skip instruction on this standard because most students are proficient (increasing the time available for other standards).

- Extend students' learning by working with them on writing paragraphs using a simile or metaphor.

- Look at the sixth-grade standard, which expects students to be able to understand and use personification as a form of figurative language.

The fifth-grade team also met with the fourth- and sixth-grade teams at the school and began looking at how the standard articulated vertically across grade levels. It collectively decided that option two, in which students would be expected to show deeper understanding of simile and metaphor and communicate their understanding within writing, would support student learning at a higher level in multiple areas.

This scenario shows a team creating system change that that will impact student learning. Throughout this process, three grade-level teams examined their practices, made refinements to their pacing guides, and identified instruction that guided students toward deeper understanding to take place across all classrooms.

The Short- and Long-Term Cycle tools in the Tools for Teams appendix (pages 117–118) can be used to remind teams of the steps they need to consider to guide this work. They start their year with the Long-Term Cycle—using the results of their external summative assessments to develop their SMART goals and action plans. They monitor their goals throughout the year to make sure their action plan is providing good results. Then, throughout each unit of instruction, they follow the steps in the Short-Term Cycle to guide them through the use of the data they gather from common formative assessments. They monitor student learning as well as their own adult learning, thus engaging in continuous improvement.

In support of this concept, we recommend that you set up a system for recording what worked and what didn't and the conclusions you came to as a result. The Considerations for the Future template (page 119) will help your team keep records of this information.

For each unit, make a note of the power standards you decided on and whether or not they ended up being the right power standards. Keep a record of the pacing decisions you made and whether or not they were appropriate as implemented. In the assessment-design box, record the reasons you chose the type of assessment and the expectations for proficiency. If there was a problem with this decision, make a note of it so that you don't use the same assessment the following year. Finally, make a record of any assessment item that was problematic. For example, were the items written at the appropriate level of rigor? Were there distracters for multiple-choice questions that didn't work? Were items ambiguous? This is information that will be important next year, but that team members are unlikely to remember in a year's time.

Celebrate Successes

This is hard work, there's no other way to say it. But it's rewarding work, and it's crucial that we celebrate the successes that result from this work at the team, school, and district level. The most obvious and direct way in which teams can celebrate is to look at the impact using common formative assessments has made on the students in their classes. Use some of these critical questions to identify your successes:

- How many students, because they were monitored and received corrective instruction, now demonstrate proficiency in learning targets that we know as educators are absolutely essential?

- Did more students demonstrate this proficiency compared to last year?

- What have we learned as a team?

- How engaged are our students in the process?

There are a number of ways in which teams and schools share the news about their successes. The AllThingsPLC website (www.allthingsplc.info) offers many ideas for celebrating within PLCs. We strongly encourage that successes are made public within schools, particularly across teams. Teacher teams will build momentum together, and the success and learning shared by one team can certainly propel others forward. We also believe it's important to share with students and parents how the use of these powerful measures is making a difference in their (or their child's) learning. Sharing successes builds shared knowledge!

A Call to Action

We hope the fact that you are reading the final chapter of this book means that you have already tried some of the steps outlined in previous chapters. We know that this process requires teams to take risks and try things they may find unfamiliar. However, the process we've laid out is intended to allow you the flexibility you need to develop and use common formative assessments that will provide you with the information you need to improve student learning.

It is important that your team continues to learn together, but it is equally important that your school and district continues to learn as well. Each year, schools and districts should come together to examine their collective results to assure that their collaborative decisions are making a difference for students. In their book *The Knowing-Doing Gap*, Pfeffer and Sutton (2000) remind us that "organizations that turn knowledge into action by not letting talk substitute for behavior are relentlessly action oriented—in their language and in ensuring through follow-up and assigning accountability that something happens as a result of talk, planning and decisions" (pp. 64–65).

We recognize that not all teachers in every school or school system are willing to immediately embrace the change that this works requires. What we do know, however, is that when teachers begin to act as though they believe all kids can learn, and they begin to see results that more and more students are learning as a result of these behaviors, they will start to change their beliefs (Pfeffer & Sutton, 2000). We encourage you, then, to get started with the work. Once you've begun to see a difference for your students as well as for yourself, we know that you will wonder why you were ever concerned about whether this was the right action to take!

You must get started in order to move forward and help others in your school and district move forward. This is the *right work* to be doing to improve student learning. We encourage you to use the materials and ideas in this book to support your work, learn together, and celebrate your successes!

APPENDIX

Tools for Teams

Work Cycle for Teams 98

SMART Goals and Action Planning Worksheet. 100

Balanced Assessment System Framework 101

Sample Agenda for Determining Power Standards 102

Sample Agenda for Unwrapping Standards 103

Unwrapping Template 104

Unwrapping Template for Backward Planning 105

Evaluating the Quality of an Assessment 106

Sample Protocol for Developing an Assessment 107

Assessment Plan 108

Pacing Guide Template. 109

Backward Planning Unit Design Template. 110

Data Team Meeting Template 112

Protocol for Data Team Meeting. 115

Student-Involved Assessment Worksheet. 116

Short-Term Cycle. 117

Long-Term Cycle 118

Considerations for the Future 119

Work Cycle for Teams

Prepare

Guiding Questions

- What norms should we follow to accomplish our team goals?

Team's Work and Products

- Group norms built through consensus and reviewed at least annually

Plan

Guiding Questions

- What is our greatest area of need, and why?

- What is our action plan for addressing this need during the year?

- What does research say about how to improve? Is there something we're doing already that we can build on?

- What data should we collect along the way to monitor the change? Do we need to design a common formative assessment?

Team's Work and Products

- Analysis of data to determine the greatest area of need and development of a SMART goal (short or long term)

- Action plan that (1) addresses identified needs and outlines how to improve learning with specific steps to take and data to gather through formative and summative measures and (2) addresses how the team will implement plans, review results, and revise practices based on findings (such as with lesson study, observations, walkthroughs, and team feedback)

Do

Guiding Questions

- How is the implementation of our plan going? Are we collecting data along the way? Do we need to learn more? Are we using agreed-on strategies and practices?

- Are any roadblocks interfering with our intervention or change in practice? How can we support each other? What resources can we use to support this implementation?

Team's Work and Products

- Implementing instruction as defined in the action plan, including common formative assessments

- Monitoring the implementation of new strategies

- Gathering interim data as defined in the action plan

Study

Guiding Questions

- What has changed in our students' learning?
- Is the rate of change what we expected? More? Less? Are we leaving anyone behind?
- To what do we attribute these changes?
- Is there other data we want to gather?

Team's Work and Products

- Examine student work, results of common assessments, and other areas to determine the impact of actions on student learning.
- Determine other information that might be needed.

Act

Guiding Questions

- Did we meet our goal? What did we learn throughout this process?
- What recommendations do we have for continuous improvement in this area?
- How can we hold the gains? What might be our next steps?
- How did we work together?

Team's Work and Products

- Determine any immediate actions or adjustments that are indicated (re-teaching, curricular adjustments, interventions).
- Develop recommendations for further work.
- Review group's performance (norms).

SMART Goals and Action Planning Worksheet

Current Reality →

Desired Reality (Our SMART Goal) →

Possible Causes for Gap Between Goal and Reality?

Action Plan and Tools for Monitoring

What is our step-by-step plan to accomplish this goal? What tools can we use (or create) to check whether students are making progress (in other words, is our plan working)?

Action Steps	Evidence of Success or Completion				

Possible Causes for Gap Between Goal and Reality?

Is the curriculum we teach truly aligned to the standards?

Are we ordering and prioritizing our instruction effectively?

Are we using formative assessment data to monitor the learning of every student? Is that information being used to adjust instruction on an ongoing basis? Are students familiar with assessment vocabulary and format?

Are we using effective teaching strategies?

Are the tools and materials we use effective in delivering our instruction?

Are we meeting the needs of our struggling students by providing additional time and support?

Desired Reality (Our SMART Goal)

What specifically will students do?

To what extent and by when?

As measured by what?

Example: By June 2004, 90 percent of our students will write a well-developed persuasive essay attaining a score of 3 as measured by our district writing rubric.

Current Reality

What is the data showing as the greatest area of need?

What specific skills and concepts must we focus on?

Balanced Assessment System Framework

	Classroom Assessments		Common Formative Assessments	Benchmark Assessments	External Summative Assessments
Examples of practice	Worksheets, clickers, whiteboards, exit slips, conferences	Final exams, final projects	Tasks assessed with rubrics, short quizzes, common worksheets, and clickers	Quarterly tests or performances, writing samples	State tests and ACT, SAT, and AP exams
Formative or summative?	Very formative	More summative	Very formative	More summative	Summative
Whose responsibility?	Classroom teachers	Classroom teachers	Collaborative teams at each school	District teams of representative teachers	An external group of experts
Purpose?	To give immediate feedback	To give a grade	To determine if students have learned the material and how to respond	To assess curriculum, instructional strategies, and pacing	To determine whether curriculum, instructional strategies, and pacing were appropriate

Sample Agenda for Determining Power Standards*

Time	Description of Activity	Product
Ten minutes	The team discusses the terms *endurance*, *leverage*, and *readiness* to make sure team members have a common understanding of these criteria and what they are looking for.	
Twenty minutes	Each team member works independently to apply the three criteria to his or her list of state standards. It is important not to take too much time during this step or some teachers may overthink the process and want to mark most of the standards.	Each teacher will have highlighted approximately one-third of his or her standards, indicating the ones he or she believes meet the criteria.
Up to an hour	During this step, the team builds consensus about which standards belong on the draft list. Team members may spend time discussing what the standard means.	Teams develop a first draft of their team list of power standards.
Twenty minutes	Compare the draft of power standards to the state blueprint indicating what is likely going to be emphasized on the state test. The team may want to spend some additional time looking at longitudinal data about how students generally do on the state test.	Teams might revise the draft to reflect what they've learned.
Thirty minutes to one hour	Teams review how their draft list of power standards fits into the standards chosen by the grade level or course before theirs and the grade level or course taught after theirs. They look for gaps and redundancies.	Each team walks away with a final list of power standards for its team that is aligned to the state test blueprint and vertically aligned with other teams in its building or district.
Varies	The team then discusses the pacing of its power standards. For some schools and districts this is done using previously developed curriculum maps or pacing guides. For others, this will take much longer if teams are starting from scratch.	Teams should have a document that lays out—at least quarterly or by trimester— which power standards are being taught during that quarter or trimester.

This will likely not all happen during the same meeting.

Sample Agenda for Unwrapping Standards

Facilitator Notes

Refresh members of the team about today's goal and the purpose and importance of unwrapping the standards.

Purpose—To get team clarity of the power standards through an examination of the skills and concepts, big ideas, and potential essential/guiding questions that they address

Why is this important?—The highest levels of learning occur when all teachers agree on the prioritized curriculum *and* when students are clear about what they're trying to learn. By unwrapping the standards, we can all make sure we're focusing on the same learning targets that are contained within the standard. This will help us create aligned instruction and common assessments.

Materials and Equipment Needed

- Copies of the power standards for the selected content area
- Unwrapping template/graphic organizer
- Reference materials (standards frameworks, taxonomies)
- Equipment and materials for the group process (document camera, overhead projector, chart paper)

Unwrapping Process

- Make sure everyone has a copy of the selected standard from the power standards.
- Ask team members to circle the key verbs (skills) and nouns (concepts) contained within the standard.
- Using the graphic organizer/template, collectively reorganize the concepts (the "need to know" nouns) and the skills (the "able to do" verbs). It's not absolutely necessary that each member of the team to use the same graphic organizer. (Facilitator note: You can do this using a document camera, an overhead projector, chart paper, or a whiteboard.)
- Identify the academic language that must be reinforced or established.
- Examine the list of identified skills, and discuss the level of thinking associated with each using the preferred taxonomy.
- Identify the big idea behind the standard.
- Identify essential questions that will lead to the big ideas and serve as a focus for instruction.

Unwrapping Template

Power Standard:		
Skills and Concepts:		
1. Students will know . . . (the concepts that support the standard)	2. And be able to . . . (the skills students are able to demonstrate after instruction)	3. Level of thinking (from one of the three frameworks listed below)
Vocabulary:		

Bloom's Taxonomy (Revised)	Marzano's Taxonomy	Webb's Depth of Knowledge
Remembering	Level 1: Retrieval	Recall and reproduction (DOK 1)
Understanding	Level 2: Comprehension	Skills and concepts (DOK 2)
Applying	Level 3: Analysis	Strategic thinking/complex reasoning (DOK 3)
Analyzing	Level 4: Knowledge utilization	Extended thinking/reasoning (DOK 4)
Evaluating	Level 5: Metacognition	
Creating	Level 6: Self-system thinking	

Unwrapping Template for Backward Planning

Guiding Questions
• What will we prioritize in our teaching during this time period or instructional unit? (Which standards or objectives?)
• What do we want students to know and be able to do at the end of this time period or instructional unit? (What are the learning targets?)
• What evidence will we see if students successfully learn these skills and concepts? (What will the assessment items show?)

Learning Targets		Level of Thinking (Bloom, Marzano, or Webb)	Type of Assessment Item (Written Response, Multiple Choice, and So On)
Concepts	Students will know . . . (simple concepts)		
	Students will know . . . (complex concepts)		
Skills	And be able to . . .		
Vocabulary that supports the standard			

Bloom's Taxonomy (Revised)	Marzano's Taxonomy	Webb's Depth of Knowledge
Remembering	Level 1: Retrieval	Recall and reproduction (DOK 1)
Understanding	Level 2: Comprehension	Skills and concepts (DOK 2)
Applying	Level 3: Analysis	Strategic thinking/complex reasoning (DOK 3)
Analyzing	Level 4: Knowledge utilization	Extended thinking/reasoning (DOK 4)
Evaluating	Level 5: Metacognition	
Creating	Level 6: Self-system thinking	

Evaluating the Quality of an Assessment

	Assessment Planning	Item Planning
Is it valid?	1. We identified specific learning targets. 2. We determined the level of rigor for each target. 3. We matched the assessment to the identified level of thinking.	1. The assessment items match the cognitive demand of the learning target. 2. Students know which items match each learning target.
Is it reliable?	1. We used a sufficient number of questions to ensure reliability (four multiple choice, one well-written constructed-response or performance assessment). 2. The team agrees with the way proficiency has been determined and how the items will be scored.	1. The reading level of the questions won't interfere with the assessment. 2. There are no give aways in selected-response items. 3. There are no ambiguous answers in selected-response items. 4. There is a context, when appropriate, for constructed-response items.

Source: Gareis and Grant, 2008; Stiggins et al., 2004

Sample Protocol for Developing an Assessment

Facilitator Notes

Remind team members that the purpose of each common formative assessment is to provide data back to the team about which students have or have not mastered each of the learning targets being assessed. The assessment needs to be short and easy enough to score so that the team can respond quickly to the results.

The team will respond to students who need additional time and support around a specific learning target, those who might benefit from additional practice, as well as those who would benefit with opportunities for enrichment and extension.

Materials Needed

- The unwrapped organizer for the standard(s)
- Template for assessment plan

The Design Process

Step One: Decide What to Assess

Consider all of the learning targets you have found during the unwrapping process that are being taught during this part of the unit. Decide which of these targets to assess. Remember you do not have to assess every learning target.

Consider:

1. Which targets are most likely to cause certain students difficulty?
2. Which targets are most important or prerequisite skills for information to come later in this unit?
3. Which targets are absolutely necessary for students to know?

Step Two: Decide How to Assess

For each learning target, make sure team members agree on the expected level of thinking for mastery of that target. For each learning target, choose the most appropriate assessment method: selected response, constructed response, or performance assessment. Make sure that the thinking level you're expecting can be assessed with the type of assessment you've chosen.

Step Three: Develop the Assessment Plan

Complete the assessment plan. Decide what type of items and how many items you will use to assess student learning on each target. Consider how long the assessment will take to administer and how much time teachers will need to score the results.

Step Four: Determine the Timeline

Decide the date or range of dates for administering the assessment and the date for the next meeting to discuss results. Remember to consider scoring time before establishing the date for the meeting to discuss the data.

Step Five: Write the Assessment

Use the guidelines for quality item writing while writing the assessment.

Step Six: Review the Assessment Before Administration

Review the assessment to make sure the directions are clear and that students will understand what you are expecting from them during the assessment.

Step Seven: Set Proficiency Criteria and Decide How to Gather the Data

Determine what the score for proficiency will be so that data can be reported back by learning target and by student.

Assessment Plan

Use one form for each assessment planned during the unit.

Assessment:

	Knowledge	Application	Analysis	Evaluation	Total Items/ Total Time
Target 1					
Target 2					
Target 3					

Key: SR = selected response; CWS = constructed or written response; P = performance assessment; Light grey = selected response may be appropriate; dark grey = selected response may not be appropriate

Timeline for Assessment	
Follow-Up Data Meeting Date	

Pacing Guide Template

Course:		Planning Team:	
Week	Day	Power Standard Focus (State the Skills or Concepts)	Materials and Lessons
1	Monday		
	Tuesday		
	Wednesday		
	Thursday		
	Friday		
2	Monday		
	Tuesday		
	Wednesday		
	Thursday		
	Friday		
3	Monday		
	Tuesday		
	Wednesday		
	Thursday		
	Friday		
4	Monday		
	Tuesday		
	Wednesday		
	Thursday		
	Friday		

Backward Planning Unit Design Template

1. What power standard(s) will we address within this unit?

   a. Student-friendly version of the power standard(s) to reference during instruction ("I will be able to . . ."):

   b. Big ideas to establish within the unit:

   c. Essential questions that guide the learning:

2. What are the unwrapped knowledge and skills and aligned formative and summative assessments for this unit?

a. Students Will Know . . . (What concepts and vocabulary support the standard?)	Formative Measures (How will we monitor student progress on these concepts and skills along the way?)	Summative Measure(s) (What culminating measure will we use to determine students' overall attainment of this concept?)
Vocabulary:		
b. And Be Able to . . . (What things should students be able to do as part of the standard?)	Formative Measures (How will we monitor student progress on these skills along the way? Are there strong and weak models we can provide to students?)	Summative Measure(s) (What culminating measure will we use to determine students' overall achievement of this skill?)

Common Formative Assessment © 2012 by Solution Tree Press • solution-tree.com
 Visit **go.solution-tree.com/assessment** to download this page.

3. What is the sequential plan for delivering instruction and monitoring learning?

Dates	Lessons and Activities	Embedded Assessment Checkpoints (Formative and Summative)

Data Team Meeting Template

Team:

Assessment Description

Targets Assessed	Type of Assessment	Proficiency Expectation

Target 1

	Number of Students Below Proficiency	Number of Students at Proficiency	Number of Students Above Proficiency
Teacher 1			
Teacher 2			
Teacher 3			
Teacher 4			

Target 2

	Number of Students Below Proficiency	Number of Students at Proficiency	Number of Students Above Proficiency
Teacher 1			
Teacher 2			
Teacher 3			
Teacher 4			

Target 3

	Number of Students Below Proficiency	Number of Students at Proficiency	Number of Students Above Proficiency
Teacher 1			
Teacher 2			
Teacher 3			
Teacher 4			

Which students need more time and support?

Target 1

	Students Identified for Intervention, Practice, or Enrichment	Planned Instructional Strategy
Additional time and support		
Additional practice		
Enrichment		

Target 2

	Students Identified for Intervention, Practice, or Enrichment	Planned Instructional Strategy
Additional time and support		
Additional practice		
Enrichment		

Target 3

	Students Identified for Intervention, Practice, or Enrichment	Planned Instructional Strategy
Additional time and support		
Additional practice		
Enrichment		

Which questions need to be reviewed?

Question Number	Concern

Which teaching strategies or pacing issues need to be discussed?

Strategy or Topic	Issue of Concern

Protocol for Data Team Meeting

Each teacher brings his or her own data to the meeting. The data should be available by learning target and by student.

Step One: How many students were below proficiency, at proficiency, and above proficiency? Use this information to decide how to regroup students for a response.

Step Two: Did any teacher have significantly better results than the other teachers? If so, consider using the instructional strategy this teacher used in the planned intervention.

Step Three: Look at the students who didn't meet proficiency. If possible, create a hypothesis about why they may not have reached expectations. Is there a deficit in prerequisite skills? Are students concrete thinkers trying to learn an abstract concept? Do students need additional vocabulary instruction?

Step Four: Using the hypotheses about students, plan how to reteach the learning target. Decide how to group students so that those who were proficient get enrichment and those who weren't get extra time and support.

Step Five: If you don't have any new strategies to use to reteach the learning target, examine best-practice literature to learn new instructional strategies.

Step Six: Determine which teachers will provide intervention to which students using which strategy.

Step Seven: Plan how you will reassess students at the end of the intervention.

Student-Involved Assessment Worksheet

1 = We see no evidence of practice in this area.

2 = We are in the process of learning and developing strategies in this area.

3 = We demonstrate partial implementation of these practices and strategies across our team.

4 = This is consistently implemented across our team.

Elements of Student-Involved Assessment	Evidence of Practice	Processes and Strategies to Increase Student-Involved Assessment
Students are clear on the learning targets. 1 2 3 4	Team develops student-friendly targets and "I can" statements.	
Students actively engage in the identification of quality indicators. 1 2 3 4	Students are involved in development of rubrics. Students generate assessments. Teacher provides exemplars and anchor papers annotated by students.	
Students engage in guided self-assessment. 1 2 3 4	Students self-monitor their understanding. Teacher models self-assessment.	
Students engage in guided peer assessment and collaboration. 1 2 3 4	Students use assessments they have generated. Students use feedback circles.	
Students engage in self-monitoring and goal setting. 1 2 3 4	Students engage in student-led conferences and goal setting, and they track their own progress.	

Total: _____/20 points

Short-Term Cycle

Plan

- Identify power standards.
- Unwrap the standards.
- Design unit assessment.
- Set short-term SMART goal for unit.
- Write the assessments.

Do

- Preassess the students.
- Determine and use instructional strategies from best practice.
- Administer common formative assessments.

Act

- Provide additional time and support or enrichment to students who need it.
- Monitor the results with additional formative assessment.

Study

- Examine the results of each assessment—collaboratively.
- Look for strengths and weaknesses in the instructional strategies used.
- Plan for how to respond to students who learned or needed enrichment.

Long-Term Cycle

Plan

- Analyze summative and longitudinal data.
- Identify the greatest area of need (GAN).
- Establish a team SMART goal.
- Develop an action plan that involves all team members.

Act

- Don't wait until the end of the year to change your action plan.
- If you reach your goal before the end of the year, choose a new goal.
- Celebrate success along the way so that you are motivated to continue.
- Be open about your learning as a team; don't hesitate to examine best-practice literature.

Do

- Implement the action plan.
- Examine the issues of time to meet as a team and time to provide response to common formative assessments.
- Determine how you will collect and analyze data.
- Consider how you will keep records of your work.

Study

- Gather data throughout the year to monitor your results.
- Review your SMART goal to make sure you are implementing your action plan.

Considerations for the Future

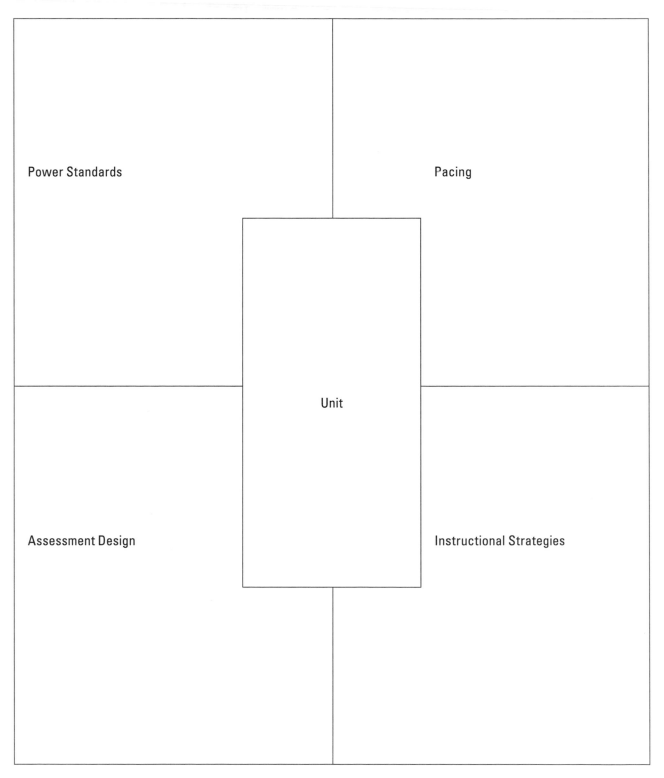

Power Standards

Pacing

Unit

Assessment Design

Instructional Strategies

REFERENCES AND RESOURCES

Ainsworth, L. (2003). *"Unwrapping" the standards: A simple process to make standards manageable.* Denver, CO: Advanced Learning Press.

Ainsworth, L. (2004). *Power standards: Identifying the standards that matter most.* Englewood, CO: Advanced Learning Press.

Ainsworth, L. (2007). Common formative assessments. In D. Reeves (Ed.), *Ahead of the curve: The power of assessment to transform teaching and learning* (pp. 79–101). Bloomington, IN: Solution Tree Press.

Ainsworth, L., & Viegut, D. (2006). Common formative assessments: How to connect standards-based instruction and assessment. Thousand Oaks, CA: Corwin Press.

Anderson, L. W., & Krathwohl, D. R. (Eds.). (2001). *A taxonomy for learning, teaching, and assessing: A revision of Bloom's Taxonomy of Educational Objectives.* Boston: Allyn & Bacon.

Arter, J., & Chappuis, J. (2006). *Creating and recognizing quality rubrics.* Portland, OR: Educational Testing Service.

Bangert-Drowns, R. L., Kulik, J. A., & Kulik, C.-L. C. (1991). Effects of frequent classroom testing. *Journal of Educational Research, 85*(2), 89–99.

Black, P., & Wiliam, D. (1998). Inside the black box: Raising standards through classroom assessment. *Phi Delta Kappan, 80*(2), 139–144, 146–148.

Brookhart, S. M. (2008). *How to give effective feedback to your students.* Alexandria, VA: Association for Supervision and Curriculum Development.

Buffum, A., Mattos, M., & Weber, C. (2009). *Pyramid response to intervention: RTI, professional learning communities, and how to respond when kids don't learn.* Bloomington, IN: Solution Tree Press.

Burney, D. (2004). Craft knowledge: The road to transforming schools. *Phi Delta Kappan, 85*(7), 526–531.

Butler, R. (1988). Enhancing and undermining intrinsic motivation; the effects of task-involving and ego-involving evaluation on interest and performance. *British Journal of Educational Psychology, 58*(1), 1–14.

California State Board of Education. (1998). *History–social science content standards for California public schools: Kindergarten through grade twelve.* Accessed at www.cde.ca.gov/be/st/ss/documents /histsoscistnd.pdf on August 24, 2011.

Chappuis, J. (2005). Helping students understand assessment. *Educational Leadership, 63*(3), 39–43.

Common Core State Standards Initiative. (2010a). About the standards. Accessed at www.corestandards .org/about-the-standards on June 28, 2011.

Common Core State Standards Initiative. (Ed.). (2010b). *Common core state standards for English language arts & literacy in history/social studies, science, and technical subjects.* Accessed at http:// corestandards.org/assets/CCSSI_ELA%20Standards.pdf on April 19, 2011.

Common Core State Standards Initiative (Ed.). (2010c). *Common core state standards for mathematics.* Accessed at http://corestandards.org/assets/CCSSI_math%20Standards.pdf on June 28, 2011.

Conzemius, A., & O'Neill, J. (2002). *The handbook for SMART school teams.* Bloomington, IN: Solution Tree Press.

Covey, S. (2004). *The 7 habits of highly effective people* (Rev. ed.). New York: Simon & Schuster.

Cox, K. (2006). *6–8 mathematics Georgia performance standards.* Atlanta, GA: Georgia Department of Education. Accessed at https://www.georgiastandards.org/Standards/Georgia%20 Performance%20Standards/Grades-6–8-Mathematics-Standards.pdf on October 16, 2010.

David, J. L. (2008). Pacing guides. *Educational Leadership, 66*(2), 87–88.

Davies, A. (2007). Involving students in the classroom assessment process. In D. Reeves (Ed.), *Ahead of the curve: The power of assessment to transform teaching and learning* (pp. 31–57). Bloomington, IN: Solution Tree Press.

DuFour, R. (2004). What is a "professional learning community"? *Educational Leadership, 61*(8), 1–6.

DuFour, R. (2010, October 27). Grading formative and summative assessments [Web log post]. Accessed at www.allthingsplc.info/wordpress/?p=1032 on April 19, 2011.

DuFour, R., DuFour, R., & Eaker, R. (2008). *Revisiting professional learning communities at work: New insights for improving schools.* Bloomington, IN: Solution Tree Press.

DuFour, R., DuFour, R., Eaker, R., & Karhanek, G. (2010). *Raising the bar and closing the gap: Whatever it takes.* Bloomington, IN: Solution Tree Press.

DuFour, R., DuFour, R., Eaker, R., & Many, T. (2010a). *Learning by doing: A handbook for professional learning communities at work* (2nd ed.). Bloomington, IN: Solution Tree Press.

DuFour, R., DuFour, R., Eaker, R., & Many, T. (2010b). *Professional learning community glossary of key terms and concepts.* Accessed at www.allthingsplc.info/pdf/links/terms.pdf on May 22, 2011.

DuFour, R., & Eaker, R. (1998). *Professional learning communities at work: Best practices for enhancing student achievement.* Bloomington, IN: Solution Tree Press.

Erkens, C., Jakicic, C., Jessie, L. G., King, D., Kramer, S. V., Many, T. M., et al. (2008). *The collaborative teacher: Working together as a professional learning community.* Bloomington, IN: Solution Tree Press.

Fullan, M. (2002). The change leader. *Educational Leadership, 59*(8), 16–21.

Fullan, M. (2008). *The six secrets of change: What the best leaders do to help their organizations survive and thrive.* San Francisco: Jossey-Bass.

Gareis, C. R., & Grant, L. W. (2008). *Teacher-made assessments: How to connect curriculum, instruction, and student learning.* Larchmont, NY: Eye on Education.

Goertz, M. E., Olah, L. N., & Riggan, M. (2009, December). *Can interim assessments be used for instructional change?* (Policy Brief No. RB-51). Philadelphia: University of Pennsylvania, Graduate School of Education, Consortium for Policy Research in Education.

Graham, P., & Ferriter, B. (2008). One step at a time. *Journal of Staff Development, 29*(3), 38–42.

Hattie, J. (2009). *Visible learning: A synthesis of over 800 meta-analyses relating to achievement.* London: Routledge.

Hess, F. M. (2008). The new stupid. *Educational Leadership, 66*(4), 12–17.

Illinois Learning Standards for Science. (2011). Accessed at http://isbe.state.il.us/ils/science/standards.htm on June 28, 2011.

Kauffman, D., Johnson, S. M., Kardos, S. M., Liu, E., & Peske, H. G. (2002). Lost at sea: New teachers' experiences with curriculum and assessment. *Teachers College Record, 104*(2), 273–300.

Kopriva, R. (2008). What's wrong with wrong answers? *Harvard Education Letter, 24*(4), 6–8.

Marzano, R. J. (2000). *Designing a new taxonomy of educational objectives.* Thousand Oaks, CA: Corwin Press.

Marzano, R. J. (2003). *What works in schools: Translating research into action.* Alexandria, VA: Association for Supervision and Curriculum Development.

Marzano, R. J. (2006). *Classroom assessment and grading that work.* Alexandria, VA: Association for Supervision and Curriculum Development.

Marzano, R. J. (2007). *The art and science of teaching: A comprehensive framework for effective instruction.* Alexandria, VA: Association for Supervision and Curriculum Development.

Marzano, R. J. (2010). *Formative assessment and standards-based grading.* Bloomington, IN: Marzano Research Laboratory.

Marzano, R. J., & Kendall, J. S. (1998). *Awash in a sea of standards.* Aurora, CO: Mid-continent Research for Education and Learning. Accessed at www.mcrel.org on September 25, 2007.

Marzano, R. J., Pickering, D. J., & Pollock, J. E. (2001). *Classroom instruction that works: Research-based strategies for increasing student achievement.* Alexandria, VA: Association for Supervision and Curriculum Development.

Massachusetts Department of Education. (2003). *Massachusetts history and social science curriculum framework.* Accessed at www.doe.mass.edu/frameworks/hss/final.pdf on June 28, 2011.

Moss, C. M., & Brookhart, S. M. (2009). *Advancing formative assessment in every classroom: A guide for instructional leaders.* Alexandria, VA: Association for Supervision and Curriculum Development.

Newmann, F. M., & Wehlage, G. (Eds.). (1995). *Successful school restructuring: Highlights of findings.* Madison: University of Wisconsin, Center on the Organization and Restructuring of Schools.

North Dakota Department of Public Instruction. (2007). *North Dakota content and achievement standards: Social studies—Grade 5.* Accessed at www.dpi.state.nd.us/standard/content/sstudies/grade5.pdf on August 24, 2011.

O'Connor, K. (2007). *A repair kit for grading: 15 fixes for broken grades.* Portland, OR: Educational Testing Service.

O'Neill, J., & Conzemius, A. (2006). *The power of SMART goals: Using goals to improve student learning.* Bloomington IN: Solution Tree Press.

Partnership for 21st Century Skills. (2009). *The MILE guide: Milestones for improving learning and education.* Washington, DC: Author.

Pfeffer, J., & Sutton, R. I. (2000). *The knowing-doing gap: How smart companies turn knowledge into action.* Boston: Harvard Business School Press.

Popham, W. J. (2003). *Test better, teach better: the instructional role of assessment.* Alexandria, VA: Association for Supervision and Curriculum Development.

Popham, W. J. (2006). Phony formative assessments: Buyer beware! *Educational Leadership, 64*(3), 86–87.

Popham, W. J. (2008a). Anchoring down the data. *Educational Leadership, 66*(4), 85–86.

Popham, W. J. (2008b). *Transformative assessment.* Alexandria, VA: Association of Supervision and Curriculum Development.

Reeves, D. B. (2002). *The leader's guide to standards: A blueprint for educational equity and excellence.* San Francisco: Jossey-Bass.

Reeves, D. (2007). Challenges and choices: the role of educational leaders in effective assessment. In D. Reeves (Ed.), *Ahead of the curve: The power of assessment to transform teaching and learning* (pp. 227–251). Bloomington, IN: Solution Tree Press.

Reeves, D. (2009). *Leading change in your school: How to conquer myths, build commitment, and get results.* Alexandria, VA: Association for Supervision and Curriculum Development.

Schmoker, M. (1999). *Results: The key to continuous school improvement* (2nd ed.). Alexandria, VA: Association for Supervision and Curriculum Development.

Schmoker, M. (2003). First things first: Demystifying data analysis. *Educational Leadership, 60*(5), 22–24.

Schmoker, M. (2006). *Results now: How we can achieve unprecedented improvements in teaching and learning.* Alexandria, VA: Association for Supervision and Curriculum Development.

Schmoker, M., & Marzano, R. (1999). Realizing the promise of standards-based education. *Educational Leadership, 56,* 17–21. Accessed at www.ascd.org on October 1, 2007.

Senge, P. M. (1990). *The fifth discipline: The art and practice of the learning organization.* New York: Doubleday/Currency.

Shepard, L. A. (2005). Linking formative assessment to scaffolding. *Educational Leadership, 63*(3), 66–70.

Steele, J. L., & Boudett, K. P. (2008). The collaborative advantage. *Educational Leadership, 66*(4), 54–59.

Stiggins, R. J., Arter, J. A., Chappuis, J., & Chappuis, S. (2004). *Classroom assessment for student learning: Doing it right—Using it well.* Portland, OR: Assessment Training Institute.

Texas Education Agency. (2010). *Chapter 113: Texas essential knowledge and skills for social studies—Subchapter B, middle school.* Accessed at http://ritter.tea.state.tx.us/rules/tac/chapter113/ch113b.html on August 24, 2011.

Webb, N. L. (2005). Web alignment tool. Wisconsin Center of Educational Research, University of Wisconsin-Madison. Accessed at www.wcer.wisc.edu/WAT/index.aspx on July 1, 2011.

Wellman, B., & Lipton, L. (2004). *Data-driven dialogue: A facilitator's guide to collective inquiry.* Sherman, CT: MiraVia.

Wiggins, G. (2006, April). Healthier testing made easy: The idea of authentic assessment. *Edutopia.* Accessed at www.edutopia.org/healthiertesting-made-easy on July 1, 2010.

Wiggins, G., & McTighe, J. (2005). *Understanding by design* (2nd ed.). Alexandria, VA: Association for Supervision and Curriculum Development.

Wiliam, D. (2007). Changing classroom practice. *Educational Leadership, 65*(4), 36–42.

INDEX

A

Ainsworth, L., 22, 30, 31, 33–34, 35, 40, 42
AllThingsPLC, 6, 82, 96
analytic rubrics, 60
assessments
  See also common formative assessment
  balanced systems, 19–23, 101
  benchmark, 19, 21–22, 101
  classroom, 19–21, 101
  constructed/extended response, 52–53
  external summative, 19, 22, 101
  formative versus summative, 14–16
  performance, 52, 58
  plan, developing, 53–55, 108
  selected-response, 51, 52
  writing, 56–60

B

backward planning of instructional units, 68–71, 110–111
balanced assessment systems, 19–23, 101
benchmark assessments, 19, 21–22, 101
Best Hopes/Worst Fears activity, 82
Black, P., 18, 85, 88
Bloom's Taxonomy for Learning, 44
Brookhart, S., 86, 88

C

classroom assessments, 19–21, 101
collaboration
  culture of, 4
  finding time for, 5–6
Collaborative Teacher: Working Together as a Professional Learning Community, The (Erkens), 3

collaborative teams
  commitment, 6, 10
  consensus-building strategies, 8–9, 31–33
  decision making, consensual, 28–29
  fundamentals of, 5–10
  goals/mission, 6, 11–12
  how to start, 10–12
  meeting protocol, 114
  meetings, strategies for running organized and efficient, 10–11
  meeting template, 112–114
  norms, 7–8
  PDSA (plan, do, study, act) model, 6–7, 92, 93
  products, development of purposeful, 10
  role of, in professional learning communities, 5
  support, 92–93
collective inquiry, 6
commitment, collaboration and, 6, 10
Common Core State Standards, 15, 20, 30, 39, 40
  power standards and, 34–35
common formative assessment
  See also designing common formative assessments
  benefits of, 16–18, 21, 92
  data, gathering and collecting, 24–25, 74–75
  defined, 16
  grading, 23–24
  reviewing, 79–80
  time needed to create, 23

consensus-building strategies, 8–9, 31–33
constructed-response items, 52–53, 58
continuous improvement
  benefits, 92
  experience, role of, 94
  focused, need to be, 92
  future template, 119
  immediate and systemic learning, attention to, 94–85
  leadership 93–94
  Short- and Long-Term Cycle Tools, 117–118
  successes, identifying, 95–96
  team support, 92–93
corrective instruction, 17
  finding time for, 80–81
  how to provide, 78
  resources for providing, 78–79
  Tier 2 response, 81–82
Covey, S., 68
curriculum, viable, 38

D

data
  analyzing, 75–76
  gathering and collecting, 24–25, 74–75
  planning response using, 76–79
  team meeting protocol, 115
  team meeting template, 112–114
David, J., 64
decision making
  analyzing data, 75–76
  gathering and collecting data, 24–25, 74–75

decision making (*continued*)
    planning response, 76–79
    reviewing assessment, 79–80
    team meeting protocol, 115
    team meeting template, 112–114
declarative knowledge, 39–40
deconstructing, 38
Depth of Knowledge, 44
designing common formative
        assessments
    assessment plan, developing, 53–55
    data collection, planning for, 60–61
    evaluation tool, 106
    how to assess, 51–53
    items, number of, 55
    proficiency criteria, 60
    protocol for developing an assessment
        tool, 107
    reviewing, 60
    rubrics, 54–55, 60
    timeline, 56
    what to assess, 50–51
    writing assessment, 56–60
districtwide power standards, 35–36
DuFour, R., 3, 4, 5, 14, 16, 24, 76, 92

E

Eaker, R., 3, 5, 14, 16
endurance, 30
equity, 17
essential learning. *See* power standards
extended-response items, 52–53, 58
external summative assessments, 19, 22,
        101

F

feedback, 24, 87–88
Fist to Five strategy, 9
formative versus summative assessments,
        14–16
future considerations, 119

G

goals/mission
    collaboration and, 6, 11–12
    SMART, 7, 12, 100
grading, 23–24
guided questions, establishing, 45

H

Hattie, J., 5, 87, 89
holistic rubrics, 60

I

I do/We do/You do approach, 88–89
improvement. *See* continuous
        improvement
"Inside the Black Box" (Black and
        Wiliam), 88
instructional units, backward planning,
        68–71, 110–111
intervention planning, pacing guides
        and 66–67

K

Kendall, J. S., 27
Knowing-Doing Gap, The (Pfeffer and
        Sutton), 96
knowledge, declarative versus
        procedural, 39–40

L

leadership, 93–94
learning
    focus on, 4
    visible, 5, 89
*Learning by Doing: A Handbook for
        Professional Learning Communities
        at Work* (DuFour, DuFour, Eaker,
        and Many), 3, 8, 10
learning/lesson plans, backward
        planning, 68–71
learning targets
    analysis of level of thinking, 44–45
    clarify unmeasurable, 43
    defined, 15
    identify implied, 42–43
    unwrapping standards, 40–47
leverage, 30
Lipton, L., 82
Long-Term Cycle Tools, 118

M

Many, T., 3, 14, 16
Marzano, R., 27, 28, 38, 52, 54–55, 78
    Taxonomy, 44
McTighe, J., 38, 45, 68
meetings
    agendas, 11
    roles for, 11
    strategies for running organized and
        efficient, 10–11
    template, 112–114
Moss, C. M., 86

N

norms, team, 7–8

O

O'Connor, K., 23–24

P

pacing guides
    developing, 64–68
    graphic organizers for, 66, 67
    intervention planning and 66–67
    purpose of, 64
    sources of information on, 65
    template, 109
PDSA (plan, do, study, act) model, 6–7,
        92, 93
performance assessments, 52, 58
personal communication, 52
Pfeffer, J., 96
Popham, J., 18, 38, 84, 92
power standards
    agenda for determining, 102
    aligning, 33–34
    Common Core State Standards, role
        of, 34–35
    criteria for determining, 30–31
    defined, 29–30
    essential learning, defined, 30–31
    revising, 36
    schoolwide versus districtwide, 35–36
    structure of, 38–40
    team consensus, 31–33
    terms, use of, 30
    time allowed for teaching, 35
    unwrapping, 40–47, 103
probing discussions, 52
procedural knowledge, 40
products, development of purposeful, 10
professional learning communities
        (PLCs)
    defined, 3–4
    principles of, 4
    resources on, 3
    role of teams in, 5, 13
Professional Learning Communities at
        Work, 3
proficiency criteria, 60
protocol, use of term, 10

R

*Raising the Bar and Closing the Gap:
        Whatever It Takes* (DuFour,
        DuFour, Eaker, and Karhanek), 3
readiness, 30–31
Reeves, D., 14, 29, 30, 33–34, 49
reliable, 50
response, planning, 76–79

response to intervention (RTI) model, 18

results, focus on, 4

reviewing assessment, 79–80

Revisiting Professional Learning Communities at Work: New Insights for Improving Schools (DuFour, DuFour, and Eaker), 3, 92

rubrics
  analytic, 60
  assessment design and, 54–55, 60
  defining quality work and, 86–87
  holistic, 60

S

safe environment for teams, 82

Schmoker, M., 28, 74

schoolwide power standards, 35–36

selected- response items, 51, 52, 56–58

self-reporting, 87–88

Short-Term Cycle Tools, 117

SMART goals, 7, 12, 100

standards, 15, 20
  See also Common Core State Standards; power standards

Stiggins, R. J., 38, 52–53, 55, 58, 85–86

student involvement
  assessment worksheet, 116
  defining quality work, 86–87
  feedback and self-reporting, 87–88
  how to, 85–86
  I do/We do/You do approach, 88–89
  importance of, 83–85
  rubrics, use of, 86–87

summative assessments
  external, 19, 22, 101
  formative versus, 14–16

supply response, 52

Sutton, R. I., 96

T

teamwork. *See* collaborative teams

Tier 2 response, 81–82

21st century skills, designing instruction for, 71–72

U

Understanding by Design (Wiggins and McTighe), 45

unit design, backward planning, 68–71

unpacking, 38

unwrapping standards
  agenda for, 103
  analysis of learning target's level of thinking, 44–45
  big ideas, determining, 45
  guided questions, establishing, 45
  key words/skills, identifying, 40–41
  key words/skills, organizing, 41–44
  summary of, 46
  templates, 104, 105

V

valid, 50

visible learning, 5, 89

Visible Learning: A Synthesis of Over 800 Meta-Analyses Relating to Achievement (Hattie), 5

W

Webb's Depth of Knowledge, 44

Wellman, B., 82

What Works In Schools (Marzano), 28

Wiggins, G., 18, 38, 45, 68

Wiliam, D., 18, 85, 88

Work Cycle for Teams, 7, 98

writing assessments, 56–60

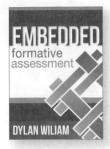

Embedded Formative Assessment
Dylan Wiliam
Formative assessment plays an important role in increasing teacher quality and student learning when it's viewed as a process rather than a tool. Emphasizing the instructional side of formative assessment, this book explores in depth the use of classroom questioning, learning intentions and success criteria, feedback, collaborative and cooperative learning, and self-regulated learning to engineer effective learning environments for students. **BKF418**

Using Formative Assessment in the RTI Framework
Kay Burke and Eileen Depka
RTI and formative assessment have the potential to positively impact student achievement. Understand the basics of RTI and its connection to formative assessment, and base instructional decisions on the results of effective formative assessment practices. Learn how to adjust instruction to increase levels of student understanding and achievement with the information, tools, and techniques presented in this practical guide. **BKF369**

Learning by Doing: A Handbook for Professional Learning Communities at Work™ (Second Edition)
Richard DuFour, Rebecca DuFour, Robert Eaker, and Thomas Many
The second edition of *Learning by Doing* is an action guide for closing the knowing-doing gap and transforming schools into PLCs. It also includes seven major additions that equip educators with essential tools for confronting challenges. **BKF416**

The Teacher as Assessment Leader
Edited by Thomas R. Guskey
Meaningful examples, expert research, and real-life experiences illustrate the capacity and responsibility every educator has to ignite positive change. Packed with practical strategies for designing, analyzing, and using assessments, this book shows how to turn best practices into usable solutions. **BKF345**

The Collaborative Teacher: Working Together as a Professional Learning Community
Cassandra Erkens, Chris Jakicic, Lillie G. Jessie, Dennis King, Sharon V. Kramer, Thomas W. Many, Mary Ann Ranells, Ainsley B. Rose, Susan K. Sparks, and Eric Twadell
Transform education from inside the classroom with this accessible anthology. Specific techniques, supporting research, and real classroom stories illustrate how to work together to create a guaranteed and viable curriculum and use data to inform instruction. **BKF257**

Visit solution-tree.com or call 800.733.6786 to order.